EXPLORE
TRANSPORTATION!

Anita Yasuda
ILLUSTRATED BY BRYAN STONE

green press INITIATIVE

Nomad Press is committed to preserving ancient forests and natural resources. We elected to print Explore Transportation! on 50% post consumer recycled paper, processed chlorine free. As a result, for this printing, we have saved:

12 Trees (40' tall and 6-8" diameter)
4,921 Gallons of Wastewater
1,979 Kilowatt Hours of Electricity
542 Pounds of Solid Waste
1,066 Pounds of Greenhouse Gases

Nomad Press made this paper choice because our printer, Thomson-Shore, Inc., is a member of Green Press Initiative, a nonprofit program dedicated to supporting authors, publishers, and suppliers in their efforts to reduce their use of fiber obtained from endangered forests.

For more information, visit www.greenpressinitiative.org.

This book was manufactured by Thomson Shore, Dexter, Michigan, USA
October 2009, Job #563LS395
ISBN: 978-1-9346704-5-3

Illustrations by Bryan Stone

Questions regarding the ordering of this book should be addressed to
Independent Publishers Group
814 N. Franklin St.
Chicago, IL 60610
www.ipgbook.com

Nomad Press
2456 Christian St.
White River Junction, VT 05001

FSC
Mixed Sources
Product group from well-managed forests, controlled sources and recycled wood or fiber
Cert no. SW-COC-002673
www.fsc.org
© 1996 Forest Stewardship Council

"This logo identifies paper that meets the standards of the Forest Stewardship Council. FSC is widely regarded as the best practice in forest management, ensuring the highest protections for forests and indigenous peoples."

Contents

LET'S EXPLORE TRANSPORTATION!

Moving People & Things by Land, Sea and Sky

Have you ever stopped to think about what life would be like without ways to move people and things from one place to another? What if the wheel hadn't been invented? How would we get around?

We would have to use our own two feet, or those of an animal. There would be no cars, trains, or airplanes to get us and our stuff where we needed to go. No bikes, motorcycles, or roller skates either. All of these ways of moving rely on the wheel. No wonder people think the wheel is the coolest thing ever invented.

TRANSPORTATION is part of our everyday life. If you have ever received a package or taken a vacation, then you have used transportation. We transport **CARGO**, food, people, and letters faster and farther than our **ANCESTORS** ever thought possible. At one time it took a few weeks by ship to get from Europe to the United States. Now it takes a few hours by plane. All of the advances we have made in transportation have made our very big world seem very, very small.

As you travel through this book, you'll learn about all types of transportation. You'll see how ancient people got around, and how animals are still used for transportation today. You'll learn how a car engine works, and what transportation might be like in the future. You'll detour through experiments that will help you understand things like why an object sinks or floats. You'll drop by to say hello to a few of the people whose inventions led to transportation as we know it today. You'll even make a backpack and a compass for the journey.

Whether it's across the ocean, the country, or just across the street, people have always been on the move. Are you ready to learn about transportation? Let's get going!

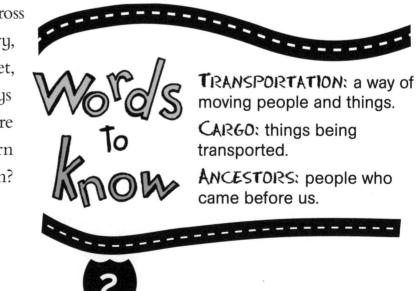

Words To Know

TRANSPORTATION: a way of moving people and things.

CARGO: things being transported.

ANCESTORS: people who came before us.

Make a Draw String Backpack

A backpack is a great way to carry around the things you need for a trip, whether you're going just around the corner or all the way to China. Some good things to carry in your backpack are a pen or pencil, a small pad of paper, tissues, sunscreen, and a quick and easy snack.

1 Cut the open end of the pillowcase so that it measures about 24 inches from top to bottom.

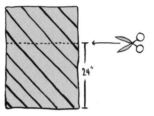

2 Turn the pillowcase inside out. Then fold over a 3-inch hem all around the part you cut.

3 Glue the hem down, all the way around, except for 1 inch. You'll need this opening for your drawstring. Let the glue dry, and then turn the pillowcase right side out.

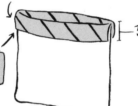

4 Fasten the safety pin to the cord and use it to help you thread the cord through the opening in the hem that you left unglued. Keep working the cord around until it has been threaded through the entire hem.

5 Glue the inch of hem you left open to insert the cord, and let it dry. Tie the two ends of the cord together. Trim the excess cord, if there is any. You want to have a long enough cord so that it creates a drawstring around the pillowcase hem, and can also hang over your shoulders.

6 Fill your backpack with things you'll need on an adventure. Drawstring your knapsack closed, and sling it over your shoulders.

SUPPLIES

→ **pillowcase**
→ **scissors**
→ **measuring tape**
→ **fabric glue**
→ **large safety pin**
→ **approximately 4 feet of cord (from a fabric or craft shop)**

Transport Yourself to Another Country

If you could go anywhere in the world, where would you go? It may not be possible for you to visit right now, but with the help of books and the Internet (ask permission first) you can transport yourself anywhere. Choose a place to visit and research the following questions. Write your ideas down in a travel journal.

1. Where would you like to go? What time of year would you travel?

2. How many different types of transportation will it take to get there?

3. What city will you arrive in? When you get there, where will you stay?

4. What will the weather be like when you arrive?

5. What special sights or attractions would you like to see during your visit?

6. How long will you stay? How will you return home?

7. How will you remember your visit?

SUPPLIES

→ **notebook for travel journal**
→ **pencil**
→ **book about another country**
→ **internet access**

Walk a Mile in Your Shoes
Transportation by Foot

People have always needed to get themselves—and their things—from one place to another. Today, our advanced forms of transportation make crossing an ocean or a country almost as easy as going to the city.

Try explaining that to a kid who lived in **PREHISTORIC** times. Back then, people only had their feet to get from one place to another, so they walked everywhere. And it was no walk in the park. Without sidewalks or paved surfaces, getting somewhere was a giant pain in the foot. Our very early ancestors walked over sharp rocks and burning hot sand, through cold puddles and slippery pools of mud.

They didn't wear sneakers. They didn't even wear shoes. Very early peoples went barefoot. Later, they wore sandals made from tree bark, wood, grass, or leaves. When they moved from one place to another,

they carried everything they owned on their backs. They even carried their houses! Because if they had to walk, it would take hours to travel just a few miles.

A Pre-Historic Walk

The first humans to arrive in what is now North America simply walked from one **CONTINENT** to another. During the **ICE AGE,** which lasted from about 2 million to 10,000 years ago, the present-day **BERING STRAIT** was covered by a bridge of land called **BERINGIA.** This land stretched from **SIBERIA** in Asia to Alaska in North America.

The first Americans were hunters who were after something to put in their stomachs. As the animals they hunted moved from one continent to another, the hunters followed them.

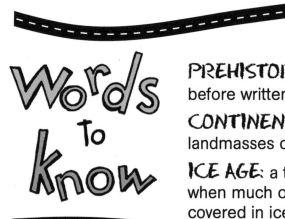

PREHISTORIC: long ago, before written history.

CONTINENTS: the major landmasses on Earth.

ICE AGE: a time in history when much of Earth was covered in ice.

BERING STRAIT: the body of water that separates Russia and Alaska.

BERINGIA: a bridge of land that covered the Bering Strait during the Ice Age.

SIBERIA: a region of Asia that is in Russia.

GRAVITY: the force that pulls objects toward each other and holds you on the earth.

Out of this World

An astronaut's space walk is also called an EVA for Extra-vehicular Activity. EVAs are an important part of space exploration. Astronauts conduct experiments and make repairs to the International Space Station. The longest EVA lasted 8 hours and 56 minutes. The astronauts who hold this record are Susan Helms and Jim Voss. Both were crew members of *Expedition* 2 in 2001. Russian cosmonaut (the Russians call their astronauts cosmonauts) Anatoly Solovyov holds the record for the most EVAs. He has walked in space 16 times.

Once they arrived in North America, some migrated south. They eventually settled in what is now Central and South America.

One Small Step . . . One Giant Leap

The most famous walk ever taken by a human occurred on July 20, 1969. That was the day that Neil Armstrong, the commander of the United States space ship, *Apollo 11*, took the first walk on the moon. He marked this historic event with the words, "that's one small step for a man, one giant leap for mankind." Commander Armstrong's walk wouldn't have been possible without a specially designed spacesuit that controlled his body's temperature and provided oxygen. Since the pull of GRAVITY on the moon is less than on the earth, Armstrong looked like he was bouncing rather than walking.

Astronauts wear special shoes that can handle all that **IMPACT**. Years after the first moonwalk, Nike designed a sports shoe that contained a shock-absorbing material like that used in the astronauts' moon boots.

There is no weather on the moon. Since there is no rain to wash them away, and no wind to blow them away, the footprints made on that first walk on the moon are still on the moon's surface.

Early Ways of Measuring

Back in the days before **CHRISTOPHER COLUMBUS** came to America, during a period in history called the Middle Ages (550-1350), European kings set the standards for measurement. Distance was measured using the king's foot. Five hundred feet between a castle and a river meant that it took 500 of the king's feet, laid heel to toe, to cover the distance. Sounds easy enough, but what if the next king had a smaller foot? Or a larger one?

Equally silly was the way early Europeans measured a yard. A king stuck out his arm and the distance between his nose and the tip of his middle finger was measured. A long nose (or a short arm) could make one king's yard different from another's.

The cubit and the span were other ways of describing distance. The cubit was the distance between the tip of the middle finger to the elbow. It usually ranged from 17 to 21 inches. The span was the length of a human hand from wrist to the tip of the middle finger. This was 6–8 inches long.

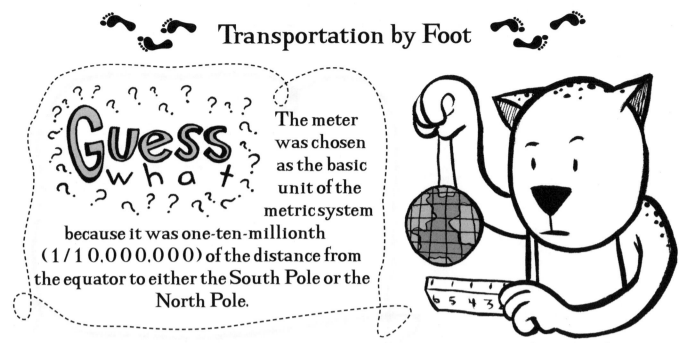

Guess what

The meter was chosen as the basic unit of the metric system because it was one-ten-millionth (1/10,000,000) of the distance from the equator to either the South Pole or the North Pole.

Over time, England **STANDARDIZED** its measurements for just about everything, including distance. Twelve inches made up 1 foot, 3 feet made a yard, and so forth. Everyone used the same standards of measurement afterwards. As colonies of England, the people in America adopted the "English System" of measurement.

The Metric System

In the International System of Units, also known as the **METRIC SYSTEM**, measurements are either evenly divided or evenly multiplied by the number 10. The metric system was developed in 1791 by a group of scientists who belonged to the French Academy of Science.

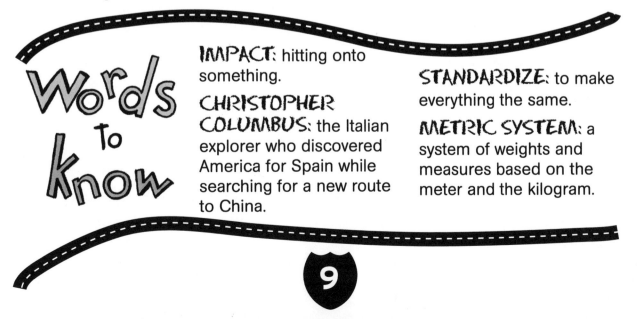

Words To Know

IMPACT: hitting onto something.

CHRISTOPHER COLUMBUS: the Italian explorer who discovered America for Spain while searching for a new route to China.

STANDARDIZE: to make everything the same.

METRIC SYSTEM: a system of weights and measures based on the meter and the kilogram.

The basic unit of measurement of the metric system is the meter. The meter's name comes from a Greek word meaning "to measure." In the metric system, you change larger units to smaller ones by multiplying by 10. One kilometer is equal to 1,000 meters. You change smaller units to larger units by dividing by 10. For example, 100 centimeters is equal to 1 meter.

The metric system was used on and off in Europe until the mid 1800s. To avoid confusion, the United States continued to use their established system of measurement based on feet and yards. At the Treaty of the Metre Conference held in Paris in 1875, a few countries decided officially to use the metric system. Still the United States resisted the change. Today, the United States is one of the few countries that does not use the metric system. Just about every other country in the world uses it.

Guess what?

In 1791, Thomas Jefferson urged Congress to adopt the METRIC SYSTEM. Congress did not take him seriously because it hadn't been adopted yet in Europe. Even France didn't officially start using the metric system until 1795.

Using Your Head

In many parts of the world, people not only use their feet to transport things, they also use their heads. INDONESIAN women, for example, carry soil, food, and vessels of water for miles by balancing them on their heads in baskets.

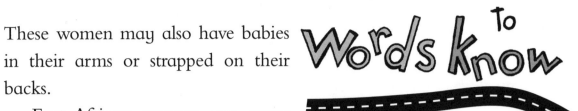

These women may also have babies in their arms or strapped on their backs.

East African women can carry loads ranging up to 20 to 70 percent of their body weight on their heads. And they do it while walking at a rate of over 2 miles per hour (3.5 kilometers per hour). Now that's really using your head!

INDONESIA: a country in the Indian and Pacific Oceans made up of almost 14,000 islands.

ROBOTICS: the science and technology of robots.

A Robot Record

In April 2008, *Ranger*, a battery-operated robot created by a team of students at Cornell University, set an unofficial world record by walking nonstop for 45 laps around the university's running track. This equaled a distance of 5.6 miles (9 kilometers). *Ranger* had four legs, AND looked like a tall sawhorse. It walked by alternating its steps between its two inside legs and its two outside legs. This made it look like a human walking with crutches. There were two purposes to the robot walk. One was to learn more about ROBOTICS. The other was to learn more about how humans walk. Information from the robot's walk will help develop artificial limbs. This will help people who have lost the ability to walk to regain their ability to move. It will also help improve the performance of athletes.

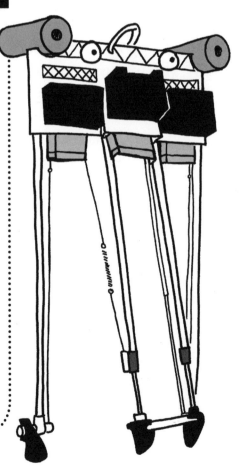

On Your Mark . . .

Racewalking has been a Summer Olympic sport since 1908. While racewalking looks like it is just fast walking, you have to follow a few rules in order to compete in a race. The first rule is that you have to have one foot on the ground at all times. Another rule is that you must keep your front leg straight while it is on the ground. To move faster, keep your **STRIDES** short and your arms close to your hips. This way you will achieve maximum **PROPULSION.**

There are two Olympic racewalking competitions: a 20-kilometer (about 12.5 miles) race for both men and women and a 50-kilometer (about 31 miles) race for men only. Racewalkers start from a standing position and the winner is determined when the racewalker's body—not just their head or foot—crosses the finish line.

Guess what

In 1 9 1 6, a canvass-topped, rubber-soled shoe called Keds became the first athletic shoe on the market. Keds quickly became known as "sneakers" because their rubber soles allowed the wearer to walk quietly and sneak around. Every other shoe at the time, except moccasins, made noise when people walked in them. Henry Nelson McKinney, a Keds salesman, is the person who gave Keds its nickname.

Words to Know

STRIDE: a step.

PROPULSION: a force that moves something.

ANTARCTICA: the land around the South Pole.

"Racing the Planet"

Each year, a group called "Racing the Planet" organizes "4 Deserts." These are foot races across four of the world's deserts. The four deserts are the salt plains of the Atacama Desert in Chile, the sand dunes of the Sahara Desert in Egypt, the icy stretches of Antarctica, and the hilly terrain of the Gobi Desert in China. Participants walk for seven days and cover 155 miles (250 kilometers). They carry everything they need for the trip on their backs, except their tents.

People "race the planet" for a number of reasons. They see remote parts of the world and meet people from different cultures. They also test their physical endurance, and raise money for charity. A few people have raced all four deserts in one year. In 2008, Dean Karnazes, a Greek-American who calls himself "Ultramarathon Man," won the 4 Deserts Series Championship for running through all four deserts in the shortest amount of time.

Guess what?

To most people, a desert is a place that is hot and dry. Therefore, it seems strange to consider ANTARCTICA a desert because it is so cold. But a desert is a place that gets little or no rainfall, does not have lakes or rivers, and can't support living vegetation, like plants and trees. Since Antarctica is all three, it is considered a desert.

Sleep Walking

Are you a somnambulist? What about a noctambulist? Both of these names describe a person who walks in his sleep. People who walk in their sleep will get out of bed and often do things that they normally do when they are awake—like eating, dressing, bathing, or even driving. When they wake up, they don't remember doing the things they did while they were asleep.

Make a Trail Mix Snack

Ancient Native Americans kept their energy level high by eating pemmican, a mixture of dried meat, berries, seeds, and melted fat. They packed this nutritious snack in leather bags made from the skin of the animals they had hunted. The trail mix you'll make is a healthy, modern version of pemmican that you can make and bring along with you to snack on during your trips.

SUPPLIES
→ large mixing bowl and spoon
→ measuring cups
→ 1/3 cup each raisins, dried apples, apricots, dates, coconut
→ 1/2 cup sesame seeds
→ 1/2 cup walnuts
→ 2 cups peanuts
→ 1 cup chocolate chips, M&M candy, or other small candy pieces
→ small plastic bags

1 Mix all of the ingredients in the mixing bowl.

2 Use the measuring cup to parcel out one-cup servings of the mixture into small plastic bags. This recipe will make about 6 bags. Don't forget to seal the bags!

A Tisket, a Tasket…You Can Make a Basket

You may not need to carry it on your head, but this papier-mâché basket is a nice way to keep or carry your belongings.

1 Blow up the balloon. Cut the newspaper into 25–30 strips about 12 inches long.

2 Pour 1 cup of the flour into the mixing bowl. Add water a little at a time until you get a thick paste. If you add too much water, add more flour. You don't want your paste to be too watery.

SUPPLIES
→ **a round balloon**
→ **old newspapers**
→ **scissors**
→ **measuring tape or ruler**
→ **1-2 cups of flour**
→ **about 1 cup of water**
→ **mixing bowl**
→ **safety pin**
→ **watercolor or tempera paints, or markers**

3 Dip each strip of newspaper into the paste mixture. Remove the excess paste from each strip by pulling it through your thumb and finger.

4 Layer the strips over the bottom half of the balloon in a weave fashion, so that it looks like a basket. If you like you can lay a few layers of strips across the top of the balloon to form a handle.

5 Put your balloon-basket in a safe place to dry. It may take several hours or overnight.

6 After the balloon is completely dry, pop the balloon with the safety pin and throw the ballon away. Paint your basket or use markers to color it.

Do the Math

Wearing good walking shoes and walking at a steady pace, the average person today can cover about 1 mile (just under 2 kilometers) in about 20 minutes. One mile equals 5,280 feet, but the number of steps it takes to walk a mile differs from person to person. How many of your steps make up a mile?

1 Measure a distance of 10 feet. Use the chalk to mark the beginning and end.

2 Walking normal steps, count how many of your steps it takes to walk from chalk mark to chalk mark. Multiply the number of steps by 528 (5,280 feet divided by the 10 feet you marked off) to get the number of your steps in a mile.

SUPPLIES

→ **measuring tape**
→ **sidewalk chalk**
→ **a parent with a car**
→ **pencil and paper**

3 Ask an adult to help you determine how far you live from your school or public library, by measuring the miles on the odometer of a car. Round up the mileage to the next largest number. Record how many miles it is. Could you walk it?

4 Do the following calculation: Using the average time of 20 minutes to walk one mile, how many minutes would it take you to walk to your school or public library? Using the number of steps it takes you to walk one mile, how many steps would you take before you reached your destination?

Beasts of Burden:
Using Animals for Transportation

It didn't take humans long to figure out that animals could help transport things. Before the technology that gave us cars, trains, and airplanes was invented, animals were the best way to help us get things from place to place.

Almost every prehistoric family had a dog, but they weren't kept as pets. They had to work. Dogs helped hunter-gatherers transport things. Dogs were harnessed to sleds, and they pulled heavy loads from camp to camp.

DONKEY

HORSE

17

Beasts of Burden

Horses, donkeys, mules, and oxen were the animals most often used as **BEASTS OF BURDEN** and **PACK ANIMALS**. Horses ran wild in prehistoric times, but by 4000 BCE they were **DOMESTICATED**. Riding bareback for long distances was uncomfortable. It was also difficult to make the horse go where you wanted it to go.

The **SYRIANS** invented the bridle around 1400 BCE and the **SCYTHIANS** invented the saddle around 500 BCE. Horses became accustomed to carrying humans, and humans got used to riding horses for long distances. Stirrups were invented much later—around 500 CE. Stirrups made it easier to mount a horse, and they gave a rider a place to rest his feet, so he wouldn't get tired quickly.

BCE/CE

Notice the letters BCE after some dates. This stands for Before Common Era. The beginning of the Common Era is marked by the birth of Jesus and begins with the year 1. Time before the first year of the Common Era is called Before Common Era. The years BCE may seem backward, because as time passes, the years actually become smaller in number. A child born in 300 BCE, for instance, would celebrate his or her 10th birthday in the year 290 BCE. Think of it as a countdown to the Common Era.

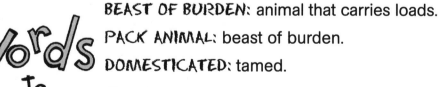

Words To Know

BEAST OF BURDEN: animal that carries loads.

PACK ANIMAL: beast of burden.

DOMESTICATED: tamed.

SYRIANS: people who live in Syria in the Middle East.

SCYTHIANS: nomadic people of ancient Iran.

OX

Animals for Transportation

The ox is a member of the cow family. Oxen are used in many countries to pull carts and plows, and haul heavy loads.

Oxen are trained to haul from a young age by a teamster, or driver. The animals learn to understand five verbal commands: get up, whoa, back up, gee (turn right) and haw (turn left).

People who use animals for ransportation often travel together in groups called caravans. Elephants, camels, llamas, donkeys, and yaks are animals that are used today for caravan travel. The camel is a good animal to use for a desert caravan because it can go for a long period of time without water. In Asia, North Africa and Australia, camel trains transport passengers and goods back and forth between stations on a set schedule, just like a regular train. Elephants are used as taxis in many Asian and African cities. These enormous animals need to drink up to 40 gallons (151 liters) of water each day.

Guess what

A camel's hump is not filled with water! It is actually made of fat and flesh. This extra fat allows camels to go without food or water for a long time. The Bactrian camel found in Central Asia has two humps and the Dromedary camel of North Africa and the Arabian countries has one.

Pack Animals and Their Countries

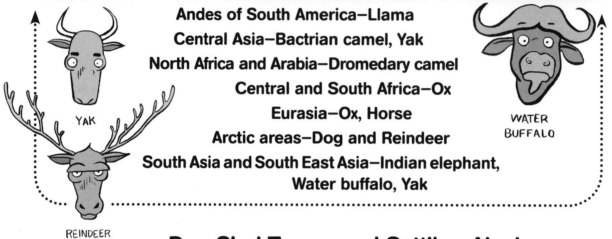

Andes of South America—Llama
Central Asia—Bactrian camel, Yak
North Africa and Arabia—Dromedary camel
Central and South Africa—Ox
Eurasia—Ox, Horse
Arctic areas—Dog and Reindeer
South Asia and South East Asia—Indian elephant,
Water buffalo, Yak

YAK

WATER BUFFALO

REINDEER

Dog Sled Teams and Settling Alaska

Until the airplane and snowmobile were invented, a dog sled was the fastest way people could travel and transport things over snow-covered, frozen ground. Dog sled teams played an important role in the settling of Alaska. Dogs pulled sleds that brought mail and **PROVISIONS** to settlers, many of whom were gold miners in western Alaska.

Guess what

The person who commands a dog sled team is called a musher. This is believed to come from the French word, marche, which means to walk.

Passengers traveled in long sleds pulled by a team of 20 dogs. Dog sled teams were such an important means of Alaskan transportation that in 1910, the United States government constructed the Iditarod Trail specifically for dog sled teams to travel between the Alaskan cities of Seward and Nome, with many stops in between.

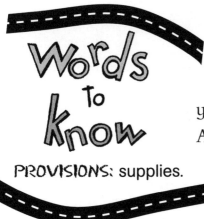

Words To Know

PROVISIONS: supplies.

The airplane and snowmobile have mostly replaced transportation by dog sleds, but the spirit of the sled dog lives on in the Iditarod Race. Each year the race starts in Anchorage, in south-central Alaska and continues to Nome on the western Bering Sea coast. Teams of 12 to 16 dogs and their musher cover over 1,150 miles in 10 to 17 days.

The Pony Express

From April 1860 to October 1861, the Pony Express delivered mail between St. Joseph, Missouri, and Sacramento, California. Here are some interesting facts about this mail delivery system:

• The Pony Express ran day and night in all kinds of weather.

• There were 165 Pony Express stations where riders changed horses.

• There were 183 riders who rode for the Pony Express.

• Riders received $100 per month.

• The youngest Pony Express rider was 11 years old and the oldest was 45 years old, but most were about 20 years old.

• Pony Express riders rode 75–100 miles before handing off the mail to another rider.

• Pony Express riders received a fresh horse every 10 to 15 miles.

• Pony Express horses traveled an average of 10 miles per hour.

Guess what

In 1933, an Alaskan musher drove a team of wolves all the way to the Chicago World's Fair to promote Alaskan statehood.

What is Horsepower?

James Watt, a Scottish inventor who improved upon the early steam engines, was the first person to use the word horsepower. He worked during the nineteenth century, when almost everyone was familiar with the horse-drawn carriage and other ways horses were used for work. Watt measured the amount of work a horse could do, and he translated this measurement into the amount of work his steam engine could perform. A steam engine that claimed to have 10 horsepower could perform the work of 10 horses. Horsepower is a term that is still used today, especially when describing motor vehicles.

Pigeon Power

Pigeons can find their way home over long distances. This makes them good for carrying messages. The message is placed into a tiny CANISTER, which is attached to the pigeon. Then the pigeon is set free. The receiver of the message watches for the pigeon to return to its nest. When the pigeon arrives, the canister is opened and the message read. Pigeons have been used to transport messages since Egyptian times.

Seeing Eye Dogs

Seeing Eye Dogs help people who cannot see well enough to get to where they need to go. German Shepherds, Labrador Retrievers, and Golden Retrievers make the best guide dogs because they are gentle and easy to train. Seeing Eye Dogs learn three commands: "forward," "left," and "right," but they will not obey these commands unless it is safe to do so. It takes months to properly train a Seeing Eye Dog, and the average dog works as a guide for about 8 years.

Words to Know

CANISTER: a container.

INTERCEPTED: stopped from getting to its destination.

CHER AMI: French for dear friend.

CROIX DE GUERRE: "cross of war" military decoration to recognise acts of bravery in war.

DUNG: animal droppings or waste.

Some of the most important messages have been carried during times of war. During World War I, pigeons carried messages when it was impossible, or too dangerous, to send them by telegraph.

A released pigeon carrying a coded message would fly to its nest behind enemy lines, where the message would be retrieved and decoded. Two-way radios were available for use on the battlefield during World War II, but messages were often **INTERCEPTED** by the enemy. So hundreds of carrier pigeons were used to transport battle plans and field positions.

The most famous war-time pigeon of all was named **"CHER AMI."** His messages saved the lives of so many American and French soldiers during World War II that France presented him with a medal called the French **"CROIX DE GUERRE."**

Yak... Yak... Yak...

The yak is used for more than just transportation. Cheese and butter are made from yak's milk. Its butter is also used as oil to light lamps. Yak fibers, which are about an inch long and come in brown, black, and white, are spun into wool for knitting, or woven into rugs and ropes. The hides are made into lightweight, oval boats called coracles. Yak **DUNG** is burned for fuel. That's a lot of yakking!

This was an important honor. General John Pershing, a U.S. Commander during World War II, is said to have presented Cher Ami with a silver medal.

One pigeon named "The Mocker" flew 52 World War I missions before it was wounded by enemy bullets. Pigeons also helped during wartime by acting as spies. They carried tiny cameras on their bodies, which photographed enemy positions.

Send a Message in a Bottle

You may not have a carrier pigeon available to transport messages for you, but you can send a message in a bottle. Be sure to get permission to do this activity.

1 Write a message that tells about your favorite subject in school and why you like it. In your message, ask the student who finds the bottle to respond by placing another message in the bottle and leaving the bottle in the same place. Sign it with your first name only. Place the note in the bottle.

2 Place the bottle somewhere in your schoolyard where another student will find it. Check every day or so until you find a new message in your bottle.

SUPPLIES
→ **a small, clean plastic soda bottle with a cap**
→ **paper and pencil.**

Guess what?
Pigeons can fly 30–59 miles (48–95 kilometers) per hour.

24

Make a Pair of Camel Bookends

SUPPLIES

→ newspaper
→ 2 bricks
→ sand-colored tempera paint
→ paintbrush
→ 12-by-12-inch pieces of felt, two colors
→ pencil
→ scissors
→ craft glue
→ black construction paper

1 Cover your work surface with newspaper. Paint the bricks and let them dry overnight.

2 After they have dried, place one brick on the felt with the smallest edge facing down. Trace an outline of the brick with the pencil. Do the same with the other brick.

3 Cut out the two pieces of felt and glue one to the bottom of each brick. The felt will protect your bookcase from the roughness of the bricks.

4 Using the template provided, trace the camel's profile on the other color of felt.

5 Cut out the templates, and glue them to the sides of each brick. You can glue the profiles so that they are both going in the same direction or so they are facing each other. Let them dry.

Merrily We Roll Along...
How the Wheel Changed Transportation

Once the wheel was invented, transportation really "got rolling." The wheel was probably invented through many small improvements over a long period of time. It didn't just come about all at once in one major invention.

Before the wheel, if people or animals couldn't carry what needed to be moved, it was dragged. At some point someone realized that things could be dragged more easily and faster if they were placed on sled–like contraption. Over time, people noticed that a log could roll.

Guess what?

The stone wheel was invented about 5,500 year ago in Mesopotamia, which is Iraq today. Spokes were added to the wheel about 800 years later.

This eventually led to the development of the sledge, a sled pulled over logs. The **SLEDGE** made moving things easier. But it wasn't faster because the logs had to be transferred from the back of the sled to the front of the sled to keep things moving.

The weight of the loads made grooves in the middle of the logs. Grooved logs seemed to make the going even faster. This led to another improvement: the **AXLE.** An axle is a thin rod on which a wheel can rotate, that is separate from the wheel. When someone attached the axle to a wooden box, the cart was born. People pulled carts before **HARNESSES** and **YOKES** were invented. Then animals were used to pull carts, which meant that people and goods could move even faster.

Chariots

The chariot was an early means of transportation that used wheels. A chariot was a small cart big enough to hold just two people—a passenger and a driver. The driver controlled a team of four horses. Other animals, like dogs, camels, and ostriches were also used to pull chariots. The ancient Romans used chariots for transportation, but they also used them for entertainment. Chariot races were held in Rome in a large sports arena called the CIRCUS MAXIMUS. Like today, crowds cheered on their teams. Chariots were also used in battles. Because it was small and fast, a chariot could move a soldier in and out of the fighting quickly.

Words to Know

SLEDGE: a large sled pulled by animals over snow or ice, or over logs.

AXLE: a thin rod a wheel turns on.

HARNESS: straps that attach a horse or other animal to a cart.

YOKE: a wooden frame for harnessing two animals to each other and to a cart or plow.

CIRCUS MAXIMUS: a large sports arena in ancient Rome.

FUN FACT

The oval tracks used for chariot races in ancient Greece and Rome were called hippodromes.

Settling the West

The invention of the wheel led to the invention of many other types of transportation. Horse-drawn carriages appeared during the 1500s. City dwellers could now be transported in a coach with two wheels, or in a four–wheeled LANDAU, or buggy. In the winter the buggies traded their wheels for runners that could go over snow and ice.

By the 1700s, enclosed stagecoaches were carrying people, mail, and money back and forth between cities. Stagecoach travelers could sit either inside or outside the coach. Racks on top of the coach held luggage. Traveling by stagecoach was a fast ride over bumpy TERRAIN. It was also dangerous. Stagecoaches were often robbed. Passengers rested and took their meals at stages, which were stations that were set up along the way.

The American pioneers who settled the West in the 1800s traveled across plains, rivers, and mountains in covered wagons. These were large and sturdy farm wagons with canvas stretched across wooden frames.

The Conestoga wagon was one type of covered wagon that transported settlers out West. It takes its name from the Conestoga Valley, which is near Lancaster, Pennsylvania. It was first used there to transport people and goods in the 1700s.

Sometimes the covered wagon was called a Prairie Schooner because the white canvas cover of the wagon looked like the sails of a ship from a distance. A covered wagon loaded with household possessions traveled at the rate of about 1–2 miles (1½ kilometers) per hour. Covered wagons weren't very comfortable to ride in, so only the very young, the very old and those who were sick rode in the wagons. Everyone else walked. A group of wagons traveling together formed a wagon train.

The Rickshaw

The rickshaw is a form of transportation that is used mainly in Asia. It is a two-wheeled cart that seats one or two people and is pulled by a person called a runner. In the past, only the rich could afford to travel in rickshaws. Today rickshaws are pulled by people on bicycles.

Bicycles

The bicycle was invented by Baron Karl von Drais de Sauerbrun, of Germany, in 1816. He called his invention a Draisine. The first bikes were wood, with a bar for steering and two wheels.

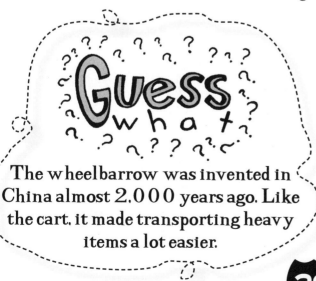

Guess what

The wheelbarrow was invented in China almost 2,000 years ago. Like the cart, it made transporting heavy items a lot easier.

Words to Know

LANDAU: horse-drawn carriage.

TERRAIN: land or ground and all of its physical features, such as hills, rocks, and water.

They didn't have pedals though, so you couldn't ride them. You sat on the seat and "walked" the bike along.

Around 1860, a French carriage-maker, Pierre Michaux, and his son, Ernest, improved

Bicycles were made out of wood, including the wheels. They had a front wheel larger than the back wheel and no pedals.

Frames are made of metal and tires are rubber and filled with air. Lots of gears and brakes make it easy to ride up and down hills and at various speeds.

the bike by attaching the pedals to a front wheel. They also designed the front wheel so that it would be slightly larger than the back wheel. The frame of the Michaux bike was iron and its wheels were made of wood rimmed in iron. Even later improvements included pedals attached to a chain with SPROCKETS and tires filled with air.

The penny-farthing was the first bicycle that could achieve speed as well as distance. It had a huge front wheel and a smaller back wheel. The penny-farthing was popular in England in Victorian times. People said its wheels looked like two British coins— the penny and the farthing—laid side by side. Men who rode penny-farthings in America were called wheelmen. Because of the height of penny-farthings, riding one required a great deal of balance. They were also difficult to stop, which made them dangerous.

Guess what?

An Olympic mountain bike competition was held for the first time in 1996, at the Summer Olympic Games in Atlanta, Georgia.

The first bicycles were called velocipedes, which means "fast foot." Most people called them "bone shakers" because riding a bike on cobblestone streets was quite a rough ride. Other names bikes have been called over the years include running machine, dandy horse, penny-farthing, ordinary, bicyclette, and high wheeler. Bicycles weren't called bicycles until 1870.

Adult-size tricycles were developed in the mid-eighteenth century. They were ridden mostly by professional men, such as doctors and lawyers, who felt riding a penny-farthing made them look foolish. Professional people liked the safety and **RESPECTABILITY** that riding a tricycle gave them. Women wore ankle-length skirts fashionable at the time, so they also found it much easier to ride a tricycle.

Other Types of Bicycles

Unicyles are one-wheeled vehicles. It takes a good deal of skill to ride a unicycle, which is why they are seen mainly at carnivals, parades, and circuses. A tandem bike is a bike ridden by more than one person. The most popular tandem bike is the twin, most commonly referred to as a "bicycle built for two." Large tandem bikes can seat 10–40 riders. A bike that seats two riders side by side is called a sociable.

A mountain bike is an all-terrain bicycle for rough dirt roads and trails. Mountain bikes have wider tires with a deeper **TREAD**, different gears, and special brakes to handle abnormal biking conditions.

Words To Know

SPROCKETS: the teeth on a wheel that engage the links of a chain.

RESPECTABILITY: a proper way of looking or acting.

TREAD: the grooves in a tire.

Tour de France

Bicycle races are held throughout Europe and the United States. The most popular is the Tour de France. This race, which is held in France and a neighboring country each year, is 2,200 miles (3,500 kilometers) long and takes 23 days to complete. The first Tour de France was held July 1–19, 1903. The race was started to get people to read a new French newspaper called *L'Auto*. The first race included 60 bicyclists. Today almost 200 racers participate. Each year, the Tour de France starts out in a different city in France, but it always ends in Paris.

Biking Around the World

In 1886 Thomas Stevens became the first cyclist to ride around the world. Stevens left San Francisco on April 22, 1884 with just a spare shirt, a pair of socks, and a raincoat that was both his tent and sleeping bag. His bike was a black-enameled penny-farthing with nickel-plated wheels. He rode 3,700 miles to Boston, arriving there on August 4, 1884. After sailing to Liverpool, England, the following April on a steam ship, Stevens bicycled through 21 countries. He returned to San Francisco in January 1887. Stevens kept a journal of his adventure in which he kept tabs of his mileage. By his own calculation, he biked 13,500 miles around the world.

Roller Skates & Skateboards

The first roller skates were designed in the early 1700s in the Netherlands. Someone nailed wooden spools to strips of wood and attached the strips to his shoes. These dry-land skates were called skeelers. The first **PATENT** for a roller skate was

32

issued in 1819. This skate was a wood sole fitted with two to four copper or wood rollers.

About 50 years later, in 1863, an American, James Plimpton, designed a pair of roller skates that had two parallel sets of wheels and rubber springs. Plimpton's design introduced us to the skates we have today. The wearer could skate around a curve, turn, and skate backward. Other skate designs included one that had four wheels all in a line—an early form of inline skates.

Skateboards were invented in the 1950s when surfers decided they wanted to surf on dry land. Someone attached a wooden board to a few clay roller skate wheels and took off. Today's modern skateboards have a swivel base platform attached to plastic wheels.

In crowded places like New York City, both roller skates and skateboards are used for transportation. People travel uptown, downtown, and across town to deliver documents, food, and messages. It takes a lot of skill to dodge cars and **PEDESTRIANS**, but on days when the traffic is backed up, roller skates and skateboards are actually a faster way to move.

Words to Know

PATENT: a document given to the inventor of something that protects them from someone copying their invention.

PEDESTRIANS: people walking to get from one place to another.

ICON: something that is special and well known for a certain reason.

The Little Red Wagon

Over the years millions of children have played with a little red wagon called the Radio Flyer. This **ICON** was invented by an Italian immigrant named Antonio Pasin, a furniture builder in his native country. Pasin turned to assembly–line technology being used in the automobile manufacturing industry to make his metal wagons. His Model #18 became his most popular wagon. Around 1933 he named it the "Radio Flyer" in honor of two relatively new inventions that were capturing America's interest—the radio and airplanes.

Make Your Own Water Compass

The compass is an important tool in transportation because it helps you find your way. If you know where north is you can figure out the other directions. You will always be pointing north when you make and use this water compass.

1 Rub the needle back and forth with the magnet for a couple of minutes. This will magnetize the needle.

2 Fill the pie plate with water. Place the checker or bottle cap on the water in the middle of the dish. Carefully lay the needle across the cap.

3 Place the pie plate on a windowsill or other level surface. Watch the needle slowly shift towards the north.

SUPPLIES

→ **magnet (the kind you put on your refrigerator will do)**
→ **sewing needle**
→ **low round dish (like a glass pie plate—don't use metal)**
→ **water**
→ **checker or bottle cap**

Decorate Your Bike

1 Using the crepe paper, decorate the spokes of your bike. Begin by taking a roll of crepe paper and tying it to the center spoke of your bike's front wheel. Weave the crepe paper under and around a spoke. Continue weaving until you have covered the entire wheel. It should take you several times around. Cut the roll and tape the end to the spoke. Repeat with the back wheel.

2 Decorate the handlebars by wrapping them with crepe paper. You can also cut strips of crepe paper from the rolls and tape them to the handlebars for streamers.

3 Tape flags to the handlebars to celebrate the Fourth of July. Hang Christmas ornaments, miniature dreidels, and Kwanza symbols to decorate for the winter holiday you celebrate. For spring, you can wrap your handlebars in garland, found at a craft store. Fill your basket with pine cones for an autumn look.

4 Tape short streamers to your bicycle seat. Tape them to the bottom of the seat so the tape doesn't show.

By Land or By Sea:
Boats

Rivers, lakes, and oceans cover a lot of the planet. There is much more water than land. A river is like a giant highway cutting through a forest. Think about how much easier it would be to float down a river than walk the same distance along the shore.

With a boat you can move quickly and easily from one place to another. People learned that water could be a good way to transport things.

Early Boats

At least 6,000 years ago the Egyptians floated rafts down the **NILE RIVER**. They made rafts out of logs or bunches of **REEDS** tied together. Poles, and later paddles, were used to steer the raft.

Animal skins laid across the raft made the trip a bit more comfortable and kept those on the raft dry.

Dugout canoes were an improvement over rafts. There was less chance of falling into the water from a dugout canoe and it was a drier way to travel. Early Native Americans made dugout canoes from large tree logs they set on fire. When the fire was put out, the charred insides of the log were scooped, or "dug out."

Later canoes had frames made from tree branches covered with bark and animal skins. The coverings were sewn together using tree roots and painted with RESIN to make them waterproof. Wooden canoes were lighter and easier to manage in the water than the dugout canoes. Later, canoes were made of CANVAS stretched over CEDAR frames. Today canoes can be made out of many materials, including lightweight aluminum, fiberglass, plastic, or KEVLAR.

Guess what?

The oldest known canoe in the world was found in the NETHERLANDS. According to ARCHAEOLOGISTS, it was constructed sometime between 8200 and 7600 BCE.

Words to Know

NILE RIVER: a river in Africa that is one of the longest in the world.

REEDS: tall grasses.

RESIN: a sticky substance from trees.

CANVAS: a strong cloth, usually made of cotton.

CEDAR: the wood from a type of tree.

KEVLAR: a manmade fireproof substance.

NETHERLANDS: a country in Northwest Europe.

ARCHAEOLOGIST: a scientist who studies ancient people and their cultures.

By 3000 BCE the Egyptians were powering boats with oars. These are long poles with a flat blade on the end that goes into the water. The other end of the oar is attached to the side of the boat. This combination of flat blade and attachment allowed the oarsman to push harder against the water, which made the boat go faster.

Boats powered by humans alone could only go so far. The next step in the **EVOLUTION** of the boat was using the power of the wind. When wind is trapped in a boat's **SAIL**, the wind pushes the sail, and the boat goes along with it. At first sails were made from **PAPYRUS**, and later they were made of cloth.

Guess what?

A boat made by the ancient Greeks called a trireme had three rows of oars on each side. Each oar was rowed by one man. The trireme also had a sail.

The Viking Longship

The **VIKINGS** were **NORSE** explorers, **MERCHANTS**, and warriors. As far back as around 900 CE, the Vikings used **LONGSHIPS** to explore and trade over vast distances. Archaeologists believe that the Vikings may have traveled as far as Canada, all the way from Norway.

Longships were **SYMMETRICAL** in design. The identical bow and stern allowed the ship to go in the opposite direction without having to turn around. Lines of oars—between 10 and 16—stretched down both sides of the boat. Longships were light and fast. They could go in waters as shallow as 3 feet (1 meter) deep and even come ashore and dock on a beach. Eventually, the Vikings added sails to their longships, which helped the oarsmen propel the boat, especially on long trips.

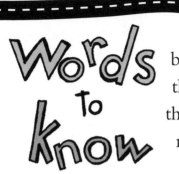

Words to Know

EVOLUTION: changing gradually over many years.

SAIL: a piece of cloth attached to the rigging of a boat that catches the wind.

PAPYRUS: a paper-like substance made from plants that grow near the Nile River.

VIKINGS: a group of people from Scandinavia.

NORSE: people living in Scandinavia in the Middle Ages.

MERCHANT: someone who buys and sells goods for profit.

LONGSHIP: light and fast boat used by the Vikings.

SYMMETRICAL: the same on both sides or ends.

CIRCUMNAVIGATE: to travel around.

CARAVEL: a sailing ship with two or three masts.

The Age of Exploration

People were curious about what lay beyond their own little world. Over the centuries they improved their boats so they could stay on the water for months at a time. Higher masts, more sails, and slimmer hulls made boats a faster way to travel. Daring adventurers, like Columbus and Magellan, made use of these improvements to explore the seas and search for new lands.

Ferdinand Magellan was the first European to sail around the world. He set sail with a crew of about 250 men from Seville, Spain, in September 1519. Magellan didn't intend to CIRCUMNAVIGATE the world. He was just searching for a shorter route from Spain to the Moluccas Islands (also called the Spice Islands) in Indonesia.

Magellan and his crew traveled west, then south around South America, on five CARAVELS. Only the *Victoria* returned to Spain with members of Magellan's crew. A storm destroyed the *Santiago, Conception* was abandoned, and the captain of the *San Antonio* deserted with his ship.

Christopher Columbus

Christopher Columbus sailed to the New World in 1492 on two different types of ships. The Santa Maria was a cargo ship called a carrack. A carrack had three or four masts and a high stern. This made it good for carrying cargo on long voyages. The Niña and Pinta were smaller ships called caravels. A caravel was a broad ship with both square and triangular sails. Caravels varied in size between 45 and 100 feet (14–30 meters) in length.

Trinidad tried to return to Spain but was captured by the Portuguese and sunk in a storm. Magellan was killed in a battle in the PHILIPPINE ISLANDS. The *Victoria* returned to Spain on September 6, 1522 with just 18 survivors of the original crew.

The Clipper Ship dominated the waters in the mid-1800s. Clipper Ships had more than 30 sails, which were unfurled to catch the wind and unleash tremendous speed. These cargo vessels were called Clipper Ships because their wind power let them "clip" (or shorten) the time it took to make a long ocean voyage between Europe, Asia, and North America. Their speed made them the most common way to transport goods all over the world. But already the age of the sail was about to come to a close. The appearance of a more powerful ship was just over the horizon.

Guess what

In 1970 a Norwegian scientist named Thor Heyerdahl sailed a papyrus boat from North Africa to the island of Barbados in the Caribbean Sea. His voyage covered a total of 2,800 miles (4,500 kilometers). He made the trip to show that early people sailing papyrus boats could have traveled long distances.

The Steam Engine

European scientists and inventors began developing an engine that could run on steam during the early 1700s. Steam is made by boiling water. The first steam-powered boats were vessels with large paddle wheels. Water was heated in a boiler until it turned into steam. The force of the steam pushed PISTONS, which turned the paddle wheels. As the paddle wheels turned, they pushed against the water. This moved the boat.

Steam engines created steam by burning coal or wood. Early steam ships had to have room to carry enough fuel for the journey, or they had to be able to dock at a location where they could obtain it.

In 1807, Robert Fulton launched the *Clermont*, the first steam-powered boat to offer passenger service. Moving at 3 to 5 miles (5 to 8 kilometers) per hour, the *Clermont* slowly chugged up the Hudson River from New York City to Albany. The 150-mile (241-kilometer) trip took 32 hours.

Paddle wheels may have been good for river travel, but it was a slow journey to take across an ocean.

Guess what

By the 1400s, Chinese junks were the largest sailing ships in the world. They were about 400 feet (122 meters) long and 150 feet (46 meters) wide. That's bigger than three football fields lined up side by side! The Chinese junk was the first ship to use waterproof compartments, called bulkheads. Junk comes from the Malayan word for boat.

Words to Know

PHILIPPINE ISLANDS: an Asian country in the Pacific ocean near Japan and China.

PISTON: a small, solid cylinder that fits into a larger, hollow one.

By the mid–1800s, propellers were introduced as a way to power ocean-going vessels. These long pieces of metal with flat blades were pushed by steam and spun underwater. As they spun around, the blades pushed the water back and the boat moved forward. Around the same time steam–driven propellers were invented, ships were beginning to be constructed from IRON instead of wood.

Words To Know

IRON: a magnetic metal found abundantly on Earth.

MAIDEN: first.

Steam Ship Firsts

The *SS Savannah* was the first American steamship to cross the Atlantic Ocean. She left Savannah, Georgia, on May 22, 1819, and arrived at Liverpool, England, on June 20, 1819. She only used steam for 88 hours of the 648 hours she was at sea. The rest of the time she used her sails. President James Monroe was aboard the *SS Savannah*, making him the first American president to travel by steamship.

In 1827, the Dutch ship *Curacao* became the first ship to cross the Atlantic Ocean powered only by steam. She traveled from Holland to the Caribbean island of Curacao. The trip took 4 weeks.

In 1845, the *SS Great Britain* became the first propeller-driven steamship to cross the Atlantic Ocean. The combination of steam and a propeller cut the time it took to cross the Atlantic Ocean from New York to London from eight weeks to 15 days!

Ocean Liners

By the twentieth century, hundreds of thousands of passengers were crossing the Atlantic Ocean each year on luxurious ocean liners. These ships were like mini-cities. They provided comfortable cabins for those who could afford them, while poorer passengers traveled in steerage. This was a tiny space at the bottom of the boat.

Guess what?

In 1840, a company called the Cunard Line launched the paddle steamer *Britannia*. They were the first to offer regular steamship service across the Atlantic Ocean. More than 160 years later, the firm is still in business, offering cruises all over the world.

One of the most well-known ocean liners was the *Titanic*, a ship built for passenger and mail service

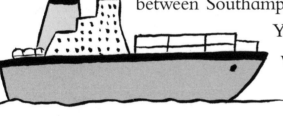

between Southampton, England, and New York City. At the time of her **MAIDEN** voyage on April 10, 1912, she was the largest and most luxurious ship ever built. The *Titanic* was also supposed to be the safest ship ever built. But during the night of April 14, the *Titanic* hit an iceberg and sank off the coast of Newfoundland. There were not enough lifeboats for all the passengers, and 1,517 people died. Only 711 were saved. As a result of the disaster, new laws regarding ocean safety were put into place.

Guess what?

Boats have names and are referred to as "she."

Submarines and Submersibles

The first **SUBMARINE** was made by a Dutch inventor named Cornelius Drebble in 1620 for King James I of England. His submarine sailed the

River Thames in England, 15 feet (4.5 meters) below the surface. Oars that poked out of flexible leather seals powered it. Air tubes above the surface allowed the oarsmen to breathe. It is said that King James I rode in one of Drebble's later models to prove it was safe.

Today a submarine **SUBMERGES** underwater by flooding special tanks located between the inner and outer hull with water. These tanks are called ballast tanks. When the submarine is ready to surface, water is pumped out of the ballast tanks. This makes the submarine lighter and forces it up to the surface. A submarine also has horizontal rudders, called diving planes, which can be tilted to help it dive and surface. Today's modern submarines run on **NUCLEAR POWER.**

Words to Know

SUBMARINE: an underwater boat.

SUBMERGE: go under water.

NUCLEAR POWER: power produced by splitting or fusing atoms.

This saves space because they don't have to carry fuel. It also means that submarines can stay out for long periods of time without running out of fuel. Submarines can go deep too—down to a depth of 2,750 feet (838 meters).

Submersibles are vessels that can travel both on the water's surface as well as below. They are used by the military and by oceanographers, scientists who study the ocean. A submersible has lights and tools. In 1985, the wreck of the *Titanic* was discovered 12,500 feet (3,810 meters) below the surface using a robot submersible called ARGO.

Hydroplanes and Hovercrafts

A hydroplane is a motorboat that travels at high speeds by skimming the surface of the water. Much of its hull stays out of the water. Australian Ken Warby is known as the "fastest man on water." In 1978, his hydroplane, Spirit of Australia, set the world's water speed record of 317 miles (511 kilometers) per hour. Spirit of Australia is now a permanent exhibit at the Australian National Maritime Museum.

In 1959, Christopher Cockerell designed the first hovercraft. A hovercraft uses fans to push air downward. Rubber skirts underneath the vessel trap this air. The air forms a cushion, which allows the hovercraft to both travel at high speeds, and hover above the water.

What Are the Parts of the Boat?

BOW—front part of the boat

CABIN—enclosed area

DECK—structure spanning the hull

HULL—internal framework covered by an outer layer

KEEL—along the center bottom, the boat's "backbone"

MAST—pole that holds the sails

PORT—left side of the boat facing forward

RIGGING—ropes that support the mast and sails

RUDDER—steering device

STARBOARD—right side of the boat facing forward

STERN—back of the boat

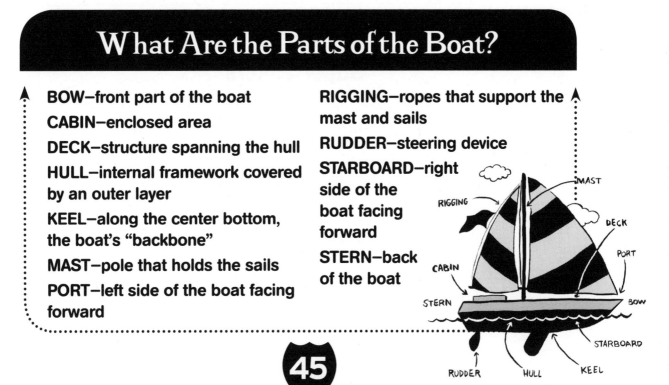

45

Ship Shape

BARGE—vessel with a flat bottom used to move freight on water.

YACHT—small boat with a triangle-shaped sail that can catch the wind from any direction and use it to propel the boat forward.

CATAMARAN—light boat with two hulls that reduce the friction between the boat and the water, so the boat travels faster. Used mostly for fun and racing.

CONTAINER SHIP—carries large containers packed with cargo. The containers are easy to load and unload. Some containers are refrigerated.

FERRY—boat that transports cars and people across rivers and lakes, and even parts of oceans.

LIFEBOAT—used by people who are shipwrecked or to rescue people who are in trouble at sea.

WATER TAXI—transports people around a harbor.

FIREBOAT—rescue boat that puts out fires on boats and on land along the shore. It pumps from the water it floats in.

Supertankers

A tank ship or "tanker" is a special ship that transports liquids—oil, chemicals, and liquefied natural gas. Oil supertankers are the largest ships in the world, as long as one-third of a mile. They weigh more than half a million tons and transport millions of gallons of oil.

The largest ship in the world, the *Nock Nevis,* is 1,504 feet (458 meters) long and 226 feet (68 meters) wide. She is so large that when full, she can't pass through the 32-mile-wide English Channel. Her cargo weighs her down so much she can't float in the shallow channel.

What Floats? What Sinks?

Any object, including a boat, will float if it weighs less than the amount of water it displaces, or pushes away. It will sink if it weighs more than the water it displaces. Here's a fun way to test some things that will sink or float because they are heavier or lighter than the water they displace. Every good scientist records his or her observations. Divide the paper into three columns. Label the columns "object," "fresh water," and "salt water."

Object	Fresh Water	Salt Water

1 Place the objects, one at a time, into the bowl of water. Observe whether they float or sink. Record your observations in the "fresh water column." Write "sink" or "float" on your chart.

2 Remove and dry off all the items. Add salt to the bowl and stir to dissolve it. Add as much salt as will dissolve. Add the items, one at a time, to the salt water. Record your observations in the column marked "salt" water.

3 Some of the items that previously sank should float, or at least float longer, in the salt water. Adding salt to the water has made it denser. This means that it is heavier in the same amount of space. The object will sink only if it is heavier than the weight of the water that it pushes aside. Some of the objects (like the penny and paper clip) will sink in both types of water. This is because they are denser than both fresh and salt water. The leaf will float in both because it is less dense than both types of water. The egg will sink in the fresh water and float in the salt water. The egg is denser than the fresh water but less dense than the salt water.

Which items are heavier than the water they displace? Which are lighter?

SUPPLIES

→ **paper and pencil**
→ **bowl of water**
→ **paper towels**
→ **ordinary table salt**
→ **spoon**

→ **common items such as a penny, checker, soda bottle cap, paper clip, leaf, popsicle stick, small straw, and an egg**

Decipher Morse Code

A distress signal is a call for help from a floating vessel or an aircraft. An SOS can be sent by Morse code, a system of signaling that uses a combination of long and short sounds. Morse code can be sent over distances using sound or light. You can write Morse code using dots and dashes, or use a flashlight to make long and short flashes of light. Try this activity with a friend.

SUPPLIES
→ paper and pencil
→ partially dark room (dark enough to see the light of the flashlight, but light enough to read)
→ 2 flashlights
→ 2 copies of Morse Code

1 Using Morse Code, create a message to send to your friend. Transmit your message using the light of the flashlight. Use a short flash for the dot and a long flash for the dash. Ask your friend to answer your message using the other flashlight.

2 What message did you send to your friend? What message did you get back?

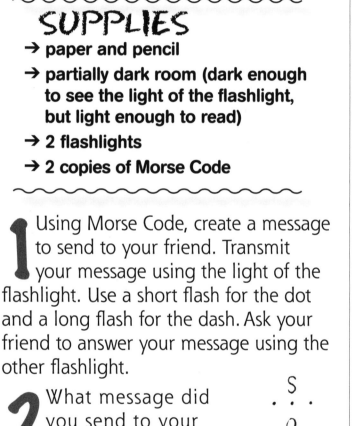

LETTERS

•–	–•••	–•–•	–••	•	••–•
a	b	c	d	e	f

––•	••••	••	•–––	–•–
g	h	i	j	k

•–••	––	–•	–––	•––•	––•–
l	m	n	o	p	q

•–•	•••	–	••–	•••–
r	s	t	u	v

•––	–••–	–•––	––••	•–•–	•––•–
w	x	y	z	ä	á

––––	••–••	––•––	–––•	••––
ch	é	ñ	ö	ü

PUNCTUATION

•–•–•–	––••––	••––••
fullstop/ period	comma	question mark

•––––•	–•–•––	–••–•
apostrophe	exclamation mark	slash

••••–	–••–•	–•–•–	•–••–•
hyphen	fraction bar	parenthesis	quotation marks

NUMBERS

•––––	••–––	•••––	••••–	•••••
1	2	3	4	5

–••••	––•••	–––••	––––•	–––––
6	7	8	9	0

Can you decipher the message below? Look for the breaks in the words.

–•–– ––– •• | •–•• ••• • | •••• •– ••• •• –• ––• | –– ––– •–• • | –•–• ••– –• •••

The Iron Rails: Trains

The same technology that improved water transportation also improved transportation by land. The United States was growing by leaps and bounds in the 1800s and people were anxious to cross the country. Covered wagons just weren't fast enough, and people turned to the Iron Horse to go from "sea to shining sea."

The **INDUSTRIAL REVOLUTION** was a period during the eighteenth and nineteenth century that saw a huge increase in **MANUFACTURING** in Europe and North America. Producing more goods meant that better and faster ways were needed to transport them. The train met this need.

49

Words To Know

INDUSTRIAL REVOLUTION: the name of the period of time that started in the late 1700s in England when machines replaced people as a way of manufacturing.

MANUFACTURING: to make large quantities of products.

TRANSCONTINENTAL: across a whole continent.

IMMIGRANT: someone settling in a new country.

Early Trains

The first trains were carts drawn by horses over wooden tracks on dirt roads. They appeared in Germany around 1550. Dirt roads were uneven, and dirty. The wooden tracks made transporting things easier and faster. Later, tracks and the cartwheels were made out of iron. The metal on metal made for a smoother ride. By 1789, wheels were being made with flanges, grooves that helped the wheel get a better grip on the rail.

Around the same time that steam technology was being used to improve transportation by sea, people were wondering if steam could also be used to run trains. In 1804, Richard Trevithick invented the Penydarren, a locomotive steam engine for trains. Steam-driven pistons drove the wheels of the locomotive to pull the train. The **PENYDARREN** was considered safer than other steam engines because its exhaust steam was drawn up the locomotive's chimney and out into the air.

Guess what?

The Pullman Sleeping Car was invented by George Pullman in 1864. This was a separate railroad car that contained small rooms with comfortable beds so that people who needed to travel overnight could get a good night's sleep.

About 25 years later, the Stockton & Darlington Railroad Company in England became the first railroad to carry both goods and passengers on regular schedules. They used a locomotive called the Rocket, which was designed by an English inventor, George Stephenson, and his son, Robert. In the United States, inventor Colonel John Stevens demonstrated the steam engine on a circular track built on his estate in Hoboken, New Jersey.

Guess what

A train's engine, called its locomotive, can both push and pull a train along a track.

The Transcontinental Railroad

In 1862, President Abraham Lincoln signed the Pacific Railroad Act into law. This act gave permission for a **TRANSCONTINENTAL** railroad to be built, and the race to connect the Atlantic and Pacific Coasts by rail was on.

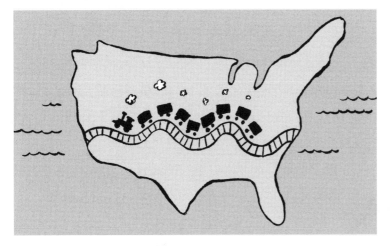

A year later, the Central Pacific Railroad began laying tracks from California to Utah. Railroad routes had already been extended from the East Coast to Chicago and St. Louis. In 1865, the Union Pacific Railroad began laying track from Utah to California.

The track was laid over 1,756 miles (2,826 kilometers) by 20,000 workers, most of them Chinese **IMMIGRANTS**. It was dangerous and often involved blasting through the rock of the Sierra Nevada Mountains of California. The two railroads met at Promontory Summit in Utah.

A ceremony honoring the driving in of the last spike to join the two railroads was held on May 10, 1869. Train service began that very day. The Transcontinental Railroad made it easier for people to travel to the West Coast of the United States. Many people settled there, and for this reason, the Transcontinental Railroad played a big part in settling the West. The train became the chief means of transporting goods and people, not only in the United States but in many other parts of the world.

More Train Improvements

In the 1890s, French engineer Rudolph Diesel invented the diesel engine. This **INTERNAL COMBUSTION ENGINE** converted coal into energy. His original model compressed hot air that set fire to coal dust and caused a series of small explosions. These explosions got pistons attached to a crankshaft moving. The movement of the pistons turned the wheels of a train and pushed it forward.

Train travel wasn't strictly diesel for long. By the 1930s, some diesel trains were being replaced by trains that ran on electricity. Today's trains contain a generator on board and are powered by a combination of a diesel engine and electricity. The diesel fuel is converted into energy, which is turned into electricity by the generator.

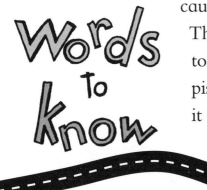

INTERNAL COMBUSTION ENGINE: an engine where fuel is burned inside a cylinder.

UNDERGROUND RAILROAD: a network of people who hid runaway slaves and helped them escape to freedom.

TGV

France's Train à Grande Vitesse (TGV for short) is the world's fastest train. On April 3, 2007, a TGV train reached a speed of 357 miles (575 kilometers) per hour. The TGV runs on electricity, and connects France with Belgium, Switzerland, and Germany. Normally the TGV reaches speeds of up to 200 miles (320 kilometers) per hour.

A Moment from History

Between 1810 and 1850, an estimated 100,000 slaves in the United States traveled to freedom in the North on the **UNDERGROUND RAILROAD**. The name came from the new form of transportation that was just getting started at the time. While trains (and boats) were sometimes used to move the runaway slaves, the Underground Railroad was mostly a network of people. They guided the slaves to safe locations where they hid until it was time to move on to the next safe location.

Many of the terms used in railroading were also used by the people running the Underground Railroad. The places where slaves were hidden were called stations. Stations were usually 10–20 miles apart. The people who hid the slaves and ran the stations were called stationmasters. A stockholder was a person who contributed money to buy food, clothing, and other necessities for the slaves. The conductor was the one responsible for moving the escapees from one station to the next.

Guess what

Early steam trains had a plow-like device in front of the engine called a cow-catcher. This piece of equipment pushed cows and other animals off the track and out of the way of the train.

Famous Train Routes

Every country has its train routes, but some routes are more popular than others. The mystery writer, Agatha Christie, brought attention to the *Orient Express* when she wrote a book in 1934 called *Murder on the Orient Express*. The first *Orient Express*, which began in 1883, was a combination of train, boat, and carriage travel.

Train Technology and Other Forms of Transportation.

- Streetcars and trolley cars run on rails set into the streets. They are powered by electricity, which they pick up from overhead cables with a PANTOGRAPH.

- Monorails are enclosed compartments that move on one rail located either above or below the track. Monorails run on electricity. Their lines are PARALLEL—as a car moves in one direction, it passes cars moving in the opposite direction.

- Subways are underground rail networks. They are powered by electricity, which could be carried along a third rail located either in the center or on the side of the other two rails.

- Snow trains have rotary snow blowers attached to the front of them. They clear snowy tracks for other trains.

- Amtrak runs an auto train, which has space for passengers' cars so that they can take their cars with them on a trip.

- Light rails are electric trains used in large cities. They take on less passengers but move at faster speeds than regular commuter trains.

- Commuter railroads bring passengers from the suburbs into large cities.

- Trains with refrigerated cars can transport food that must remain cold.

It followed a route through France, Romania, Germany, and Austria. Later the route was extended to Turkey. Another famous train route is the Trans-Siberian Railroad. This group of rail routes connects Russia with Mongolia, China, and the Sea of Japan. This railway was constructed in 1891 and runs through 7 time zones and 5,771 miles (9,288 kilometers).

Words to Know

PANTOGRAPH: a device on the roof of electric trains and locomotives for picking up electric current from overhead wires.

PARALLEL: two lines always the same distance apart.

Guess the Names of the Railroad Cars

1. I am the car most people think of when they think of a train. My name has also been associated with cardboard.

2. I am known as the "do anything" car because I will hold just about anything. I share my name with a type of transportation used in the Italian city of Venice.

3. I am one of the earliest cars to haul freight. My drop-bottom makes me good for carrying coal. My name rhymes with "copper."

4. I am open on all sides, which makes me good for carrying large loads, but since I don't have a top, my freight gets wet when it rains. I get my name from the way I look.

5. My job is to carry cars from where they are made to where they are sold. I have many levels, so I can carry hundreds of cars at a time.

6. I can carry 6500 to 32,000 gallons of liquid at one time. I fill from the top and empty from the bottom. I share my name with a super-sized boat that also carries liquids.

ANSWERS:
1. BOX CAR, 2. GONDOLA CAR, 3. HOPPER CAR, 4. FLAT CAR, 5. AUTOMOBILE RACK, 6. TANKER CAR

"The Wheels on the Bus" Traveling by Automobile

The most popular way to transport people and things today is by motor vehicle. In the United States alone there are over 250 million cars on the road.

Transporting by car started back in the 1700s when Nicholas–Joseph Cugnot, a military engineer in the French Army, hooked up a steam engine to a carriage. His invention was intended to transport cannon, and it was able to travel 3 miles (5 kilometers) per hour. Even though the steam engine was powerful, it was so heavy it made the carriage difficult to steer. Cugnot crashed his second steam carriage and destroyed it. This may have been the first known automobile crash.

Two types of engines were developed in the nineteenth century. The gasoline engine was built by the German engineer, Gottlieb Daimler, in 1883. The diesel engine was invented by the French inventor, Rudolph Diesel, in 1898. Both were internal combustion engines, which means that the combustion, or burning, took place within the engine itself. Two years

Guess what

William McKinley was the first president to ride in an automobile when he rode in a car called a Stanley Steamer in 1899.

later, Carl Benz built the first four-wheeled, gasoline-powered car called the Motorwagon. You can say that Benz was the first person ever to get a driver's license. His car was so smelly and noisy that his neighbors complained about his driving it. To keep the peace, Benz went to the local authorities to get written permission to drive his car.

While a "horseless carriage" could make life easier, most people couldn't afford to purchase one. Cars were hand crafted one at a time, which made them too expensive for the average person to afford. In 1908, Henry Ford developed a way to mass produce automobiles. Soon millions of "Model Ts" were rolling off his **ASSEMBLY LINE**.

Words to Know

ASSEMBLY LINE: a series of workstations where steps in the assembly of a product are carried out by workers or machines as the product is moved along.

THEN	NOW
Automobiles had to be hand cranked to start. Since they had no tops, drivers needed to wear goggles so that dirt from the road wouldn't get in their eyes. A driver used his hand to indicate he was turning. Headlights were kerosene lanterns.	Cars start with a key in the ignition and have directional signals called blinkers. They have automatic headlights and mandatory safety equipment like seat belts. Not only do cars have radios and CD players, some even have DVD players.

The Internal Combustion Engine

Gasoline and diesel vehicles both run on internal combustion engines. These engines convert the energy in the fuel into energy of motion. In the gas-fueled car, a mixture of fuel and air enter through an intake valve. This air-fuel mixture is compressed, or forced into less space within a cylinder.

The compressed mixture is ignited by a spark plug, which causes a small explosion. The explosion pushes pistons up and down, making a rod called a crankshaft rotate. This makes the axle, which is attached to the crankshaft, spin. When the axle spins, the wheels attached to the axle turn, moving the car.

In a diesel engine, the air is compressed first, and then the fuel is injected. The air in a diesel engine heats up when it is compressed, so no spark plug is needed.

Guess what?

Gasoline comes from oil. Oil, coal, and natural gas are called fossil fuels because the energy they contain comes from plants and animals that died millions of years ago.

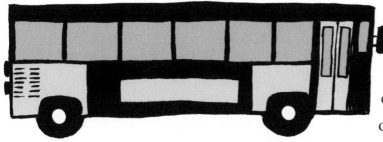

Buses

A bus is a motor vehicle that carries more than 10 passengers. The word bus comes from the Latin word, omnibus, which means "for all." The first buses were drawn by horses and later, powered by steam engines. Cities in Great Britain and Germany had motorized buses before the United States.

The first motorized bus service in the United States began around 1905 in New York City. A motorized bus was sometimes called an autobus. As automobile engine and body styles improved, so did buses. The modern bus as we know it today came about in the 1950s. Buses with two levels called doubledeckers, can transport twice as many passengers. They are popular in Europe and Asia.

A Quaker school in London was the first school to use a school bus in 1827. It was pulled by a horse and carried 25 school children. By the late 1880s, school buses were being used in the United States.

The Fastest Car in the World

The ThrustSSC is the fastest car in the world. On October 12, 1977, it reached a speed of 766 miles (1,228 kilometers) per hour. The ThrustSSC was driven by a Royal Air Force fighter pilot named Andy Green. Green raced the ThrustSSC in the Black Rock Desert of Nevada. The ThrustSSC ran on two British military fighter-bomber jet engines. The ThrustSCC's speed is the greatest achieved by any land vehicle. It was also the first land vehicle to break the sound barrier, making it the first supersonic car.

They were called "school **HACKS**," "school cars," "school trucks," or "kid hacks." They were mostly used by students who lived in rural areas where it was not possible to walk to school. In 1939, school buses became the familiar yellow color.

Trucks

Gottlieb Daimler, the inventor of the gasoline- powered engine, designed the first motor truck in 1896. Daimler's first truck could go forward and backward, and had a four-horsepower engine. Trucks began to be mass produced just before WWI.

Trucks have come a long way. Two of the first improvements were air brakes and **PNEUMATIC** tires. Today's trucks have turbo-charged diesel engines, which are more powerful than gasoline engines. Big freight haulers are heavy-duty trucks that are used for transporting

How the Jeep Got Its Name

The jeep is a light, four-wheel vehicle originally designed for the U.S. army's use during World War II. The jeep was needed for light **RECONNAISSANCE**, carrying small weapons, and transporting personnel. There are a few stories about how the jeep got its name.

One story says that the military name for the vehicle was "G.P." which stands for government purpose or general purpose. The GP was soon nicknamed "jeep." Another story says that the jeep was named after Eugene, the Jeep, a character in the Popeye cartoons. Like Eugene, the military jeep could go anywhere.

Words to know

HACK: a type of cab, short for "hackney."

PNEUMATIC: filled with air.

RECONNAISSANCE: checking out what other people are doing.

goods throughout the United States. The part of the truck that hauls the goods is called a trailer. The engine is called a tractor. The driver sits in the cab. Some cabs have beds for the driver to sleep in on long hauls. Trucks can have single or multiple trailers. If the driver's cab is directly over the engine, the truck is called a cab over. Articulated trucks can bend between the engine and the trailer.

Motorcycles

Motorcycles are a fuel-efficient way to get around. The first motorcycle was built by Gottlieb Daimler and Wilhelm Mayback in 1885. This early model looked much like a bicycle with a steam engine attached to it. A horse's saddle was used for a seat. Later motorcycles ran on gasoline engines.

Motorcycles played a big role during World War I. Their speed and small size could get them into places where other forms of military transport were too large to go. Harley Davidson has been a large manufacturer of motorcycles from the beginning. Almost 100,000 motorcycles were produced for use in World War II.

Evel Knievel was the world's most famous motorcycle stuntman. Aboard a Harley Davidson XR-750 that reached 90–100 miles (145–161 kilometers) per hour, he set world records for jumping over cars, semi-trailers, double-decker buses, aquariums with live sharks, and fountains.

In 1974, Knievel attempted to jump 1,600 feet across the Snake River Canyon in Idaho on a rocket-powered motorcycle. Soaring 2,000 feet over the canyon floor at 350 miles (563 kilometers) per hour, his parachute opened up too early and he and his bike floated to the bottom of the canyon.

Most of Knievel's stunts ended in a crash—during the course of his career he broke 433 bones. Although he was listed in the *Guinness Book of World Records* several times, Knievel never thought of himself as a daredevil. "I'm an explorer," he once told a newspaper reporter.

Under the Hood of a Car

ALTERNATOR: keeps the battery charged.

BATTERY: powers radio and lights.

CAMSHAFT: a rod that lets the engine valves open and close to let fuel in and exhaust out.

CARBURETOR: regulates the flow of air and fuel into the engine's cylinders.

CATALYTIC CONVERTER: turns harmful chemicals produced by combustion into water and carbon dioxide.

CRANKSHAFT: moves pistons, which set up a series of processes that eventually leads to the car's motion

ENGINE—converts fuel and air into energy of motion.

CYLINDER HEAD: contains an intake valve and an exhaust valve.

MUFFLER: quiets (or muffles) the sound of the engine.

PISTONS: metal cylinders sliding within tubes that exert pressure in an engine.

SPARK PLUGS: provide the initial spark to ignite the fuel in the engine.

TURBOCHARGER: compresses or pressurizes the air moving into the engine.

FUN FACT

Some countries allow transportation by road trains. These are several trailers hitched together and pulled by a single tractor. Road trains are difficult to steer and are best driven on roads that get little or no traflc.

Car Racing

The first recorded auto race on a closed track took place in September 1896 on a horse race track in Rhode Island. Three cars raced, but the distance raced is unknown. The winner had built the car himself.

The first organized automobile race occurred in February 1903 in Florida. This small event eventually became the annual Daytona 500, the race that starts off the NASCAR circuit each season.

The National Association for STOCK CAR Auto Racing (NASCAR) was founded as the National Champion Stock Car Circuit in December 1947. It was put together to organize the unstructured sport of stock car racing. The main racing car of the time was the "Modified," a car with a pre–World War II body and a modified Ford, Mercury, Cadillac, or Lincoln engine. The first season consisted of 40 events on 14 different tracks. The winner, Truman Fontello Flock, received a 4-foot-tall trophy and $1,000. Today racers drive for motor clubs that are sponsored by large businesses and corporations. The trophy is known as the Sprint Cup.

Hybrid Car

People have been using hybrid vehicles to get around for years. Any vehicle that uses a combination of two or more energy sources to achieve motion is a hybrid. Mopeds, diesel-electric trains, and nuclear submarines are all examples of hybrids. The hybrid car has two engines. One is an internal combustion engine that burns gasoline. The other uses an alternative fuel, such as electricity, compressed natural gas, liquid petroleum gas, or a **BIOFUEL.**

Most hybrid cars available today are hybrid electric. Batteries in the car provide electricity to an electric motor, which cuts down on fuel consumption. There are two types of hybrid electric cars. In one model, called the parallel hybrid, the gasoline-fired combustion engine and the electrical motor work together. In the other model, the series hybrid, the gasoline engine and the electric motor work one at a time. The gasoline engine turns a generator. The generator can then work in one of two ways. It can either charge the batteries or power the electric motor. Either model uses less gasoline, which means less **GREENHOUSE GASES** are produced. In addition, because a hybrid has an electrical engine, the car can travel farther without having to refuel.

How Can You Help?

You don't have to be old enough to drive a car to help our planet. People of all ages can do their part to cut down on pollution and greenhouse gases and save fossil fuels. What can you do to help? You might try walking to school instead of riding in the car. That's just one suggestion. Make a list of five things you can do now to help and get started today.

Guess what?

Trucks that carry hazardous materials are called trawlers. The hazardous material is transported in tanks that are clearly labeled in case of emergency.

Make a Racing Car Bookmark

1 Make a drawing of a racing car. Carefully cut it out.

SUPPLIES
→ **paper**
→ **scissors**
→ **crayons, colored pencils, or markers**

2 What do you want to name your car? Do you want the name to make you think of speed or winning, or something else? Should the name be about luck or hard work?

3 Draw the name on the side of the car. Use your imagination to color the car on both sides. You can use the bookmark to mark your place in a book, or give it away as a gift.

Create Your Own Names for Cars

Car brands all have names. The name can be used to help tell the story about the car, which helps to sell it. This is called marketing. A car name can make you think about the freedom of the open road, or feel like a movie star. Where do cars get their names?

STATES:
Chrysler New Yorker

BIRDS:
Jeep Eagle

FAMOUS CAR RACES:
Pontiac Grand Prix

CITIES:
Chrysler Newport

COWBOYS:
Jeep Wrangler

ASTROLOGICAL SIGNS: Ford Taurus

INSECTS:
Volkswagon Beetle
Alfa Romeo Spider

HORSES:
Ford Mustang
Dodge Colt
Ford Bronco

NATIVE AMERICANS:
Jeep Cherokee
Mazda Navajo

NEW YORK CITY STREET:
Chrysler Park Avenue

SUPPLIES
→ paper
→ colored pencils

1 Make a list of some of the cars you know about, especially your favorite cars. Try to come up with at least 10.

2 Think about what these names mean or where they come from. Do any of these names fall into a category? Are they the name of a place? An animal? Write this down next to each name.

3 Now think about what ideas these names communicate? Speed? Toughness? Freedom? Is the name just a made up word? If so, does the name still communicate an idea? Write this down next to the name and category.

4 It's time to invent your own names for cars. What ideas do you want your names to communicate? What features should your car have? Is your car a sports car, a minivan, or a truck? Who would drive your car—a teenager, worker, mom? Your name should make that person want to buy and drive your car.

5 Draw a picture of your car with its name. You can even make the style of the letters in the name help to communicate the idea of your car.

Make a Traffic Light Picture Frame

As the number of cars on the roads increased, so did the number of crashes. Every driver thought that he or she had the right of way. When cars came to INTERSECTIONS, no one stopped. Can you imagine what it would be like today without traffic lights to bring order to our roads? The traffic light was invented in 1912 by a Salt Lake City policeman named Lester Wire. The first traffic light had only two colors—red and green. The first three-color traffic light was used in 1920 in Michigan. There, William L. Potts, using railroad signals for a model, added the yellow color as a way to alert drivers that the lights were changing.

SUPPLIES

→ black, red, yellow, and green construction paper, 8½ by 11 inches
→ scissors
→ glass or plastic cup about 3 inches across
→ pencil
→ glue
→ three small photographs to place in your frame

1 Fold a piece of black construction paper in half. It should be tall and narrow. Cut along the fold. Using the cup, trace a circle on each of the other colors of construction paper—one in green, one in yellow and one in red construction paper. Cut them out.

2 Glue the circles on your traffic light in the order that they appear on a real traffic light, with red on top, yellow in the middle, and green on the bottom.

3 Cut your photographs to fit in the traffic light circles. Glue them on. Hang on the refrigerator or your wall, or give your traffic light picture to someone special as a gift or card.

Draw a Map of Your Neighborhood

Cartography is the art of making maps. The oldest known map was drawn by hand on a clay tablet in 2300 BCE. It is believed to be a map of the ancient city of Babylonia, located in what is now Iraq. After the invention of the printing press, maps became easier to reproduce. Maps of the world began appearing when Christopher Columbus and other explorers began charting new lands. Because areas change over time, maps change as well. What did your neighborhood look like 50 years ago? The local history section in your public library can show you how your neighborhood has changed over time. Preserve a little bit of history by creating a map of your neighborhood.

SUPPLIES
→ paper
→ several sheets of graph paper
→ colored pencils
→ tape

1 Sketch a map of your neighborhood on the plain paper. What will go on your map? How about your home, street, the homes of your neighbors and friends, any playgrounds or parks, and other interesting places. You can expand your map to include your entire city. Be sure to mark where your school, public library, house of worship, and favorite stores are located.

2 Ask a grownup to help you figure out how far apart each of these places is from one another. You can drive from place to place, recording the miles (or kilometers) as you go. This will help you understand where things are compared to each other.

3 Now draw your map on the graph paper. The blocks of the paper will help you keep everything organized. You may need to tape pieces of graph paper together to make a map that is large enough.

4 Draw a legend for your map. A legend is a picture dictionary that shows people who look at your map what the different areas are. If you have an open area on your map, show this by shading in the area, and then draw a small shaded area on your legend, next to the words "open area." Mountains or hills can be illustrated with a double M (MM). Rivers are shown with a squiggly line. Hang your map on the wall.

Make a Checkered Flag Door Hanging

When the winning car crosses the finish line at a NASCAR race, the checkered flag is waved. You'll always be a winner with a checkered flag hanging on your door.

SUPPLIES

→ white cloth, approximately 7 inches by 8 inches (18 by 20 centimeters)
→ fabric glue
→ black cloth, about ½ yard (½ meter) long
→ pencil
→ paper
→ ruler
→ scissors
→ permanent marker, any color
→ three sturdy straws
→ tape
→ about 2 feet of black or white ribbon

1 Turn over the edge of the white cloth approximately 1 inch all around. Glue it down to make a hem.

2 On a piece of paper measure a 1-inch-by-1-inch (2½ centimeter) square. This is your pattern for the black squares. Cut it out. Trace the pattern on the black cloth. Cut out 15 black squares.

3 Using fabric glue, attach the black squares to the white cloth as shown in the illustration. Let it dry. Write your name directly above or below the checkerboard pattern with the marker.

4 Carefully make two tiny slits on the top of the flag near the hem. Tape the three straws together to make one long straw. Insert them through the slits you made on the top hem of the flag. The straws should stick out on each side of the flag. Cut off any excess. Tie the ribbon to each straw and hang on your door.

Up, Up
and Away

O nce humans were traveling and transporting things by land and sea, there was now here to go but up. Flying like a bird is an idea that people had dreamed about for hundreds, even thousands of years.

Hot air balloons and airplanes came first. Spaceships soon followed. What will humans come up with next?

Hot Air Balloons

People first began reaching for the skies in hot air balloons. Two French brothers, Joseph-Michel and Jacques Etienne Montgolfier, built the first hot air balloon in 1783. Joseph got the idea from watching clothes drying by a fire.

Words to Know

BILLOW: swell or fill with air.

VERSAILLES: a large, very fancy palace near Paris.

PATENT: the right to make or sell an invention.

PROTOTYPE: the first model of something new.

He noticed that the air heated by the fire made the clothes **BILLOW**.

Using cloth that is stiff, called taffeta, and chords attached to a basket, the brothers tested their design. A burner similar to a portable grill heated air, which filled the balloon. Hot air is lighter than the air around it. The hot air made the balloon rise, and the basket rose with it.

A sheep, a duck and a rooster were the first living things sent up in a hot air balloon. The test flight took place in front of a crowd at the royal palace in **VERSAILLES**. The king and queen of France were watching also. The flight lasted approximately 8 minutes and traveled 2 miles (3 kilometers). The balloon got as high as about 1,500 feet (460 meters), then landed safely.

The Ariel Bird

In 1877, an American named James Jackson Pennington of Henryville, Tennessee, received a **PATENT** for a hot air balloon that was similar to the one invented by the Montgolfier brothers. But instead of heating the air, Pennington's flying balloon had a fan suspended from the balloon. The fan drew in the surrounding air to inflate the balloon. Then the air left through a small hole in the top of the balloon. Pennington didn't have the money to build a completed **PROTOTYPE**, and he died in 1884, before he could finish it. His widow sold the idea of the Ariel Bird to the Wright Brothers for $500.

A month later, two men—a doctor and an officer of the French army—were the first humans to travel in a hot air balloon. The balloon took off from outside of Paris, flew above Paris at about 3,000 feet (910 meters) and landed safely after 25 minutes of flight. People had taken to the skies.

Airships

Airships, such as dirigibles or blimps, were invented in 1852 in France. These early vehicles of the sky flew on hydrogen gas, a steam engine, and propellers. Airships were improved over the next 50 years. In 1901, a German count named Ferdinand von Zeppelin launched the Luftschiff Zeppelin LZ1. Von Zeppelin's airship design included a rigid frame covered with cotton cloth, and 17 **HYDROGEN**-filled gas cells, which were covered in rubber. There were forward and **AFT** rudders for steering and two, 15-horsepower Daimler engines. Each engine rotated two propellers.

Von Zeppelin's airship was named a zeppelin. It became a common way to cross the Atlantic Ocean in the years before World War II.

The largest zeppelin was the *Hindenburg*, a luxury airship that went back and forth between Germany and North America on a regular basis.

Guess what

On May 6, 1896, Samuel Langley launched an unmanned, steam-driven aircraft off a boat in the POTOMAC RIVER. He was the secretary of the SMITHSONIAN INSTITUTION. His aircraft flew for three-quarters of a mile before crashing into the water.

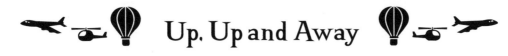

Words to Know

HYDROGEN: a gas that can be used as a fuel.

AFT: at the back.

POTOMAC RIVER: the river that goes up to Washington, D.C., our nation's capital.

SMITHSONIAN INSTITUTION: a government organization that sponsors scientific research.

FLAMMABLE: able to catch fire.

Guess what

The Goodyear Blimp and other blimps we see floating in the air today are filled with helium gas and not hydrogen gas. Helium gas is not FLAMMABLE.

The *Hindenburg* was like a hotel in the sky. Passengers slept in small rooms, ate in a nice restaurant, and relaxed in lounges and other public rooms. There was even a music salon with a grand piano. A trip from Frankfurt, Germany, to the east coast of the United States took about three days.

On May 2, 1937, as the *Hindenburg* prepared to land at Lakehurst Naval Air Station in New Jersey, it caught fire and exploded in flames. The hydrogen in its gas cells was very flammable. Thirty-six people, including one person on the ground, lost their lives. Zeppelins no longer flew after the accident.

First to Fly

Wilbur and Orville Wright were the first to make a powered, piloted airplane flight at Kitty Hawk, North Carolina, on December 17, 1903. Their plane was called *Flyer I*, and it was a glider made from birch, a lightweight wood.

The style was a biplane with two wings, one on top of the other. The **WINGSPAN** measured a little more than 40 feet (12 meters). With Orville at the rudder, *Flyer I* stayed in the air for 12 seconds and flew about 120 feet (37 meters). *Flyer I* could only seat one person at a time. Wilber got his chance to fly shortly after Orville landed.

In 1927, Charles A, Lindbergh was the first person to fly nonstop, solo, between Paris and New York. Over the next few years, airplane manufacturers worked hard to make air travel fast and comfortable.

World War II halted all transatlantic air travel trips except those that were the most necessary. Airplanes were used during the war to transport troops, supplies, and military cargo. Airplanes also played a role in the fighting when they were used to drop bombs and spy on the enemy.

After the war, faster airplanes with jet engines took to the skies. Jets like the Boeing 747 flew higher and faster and carried more passengers than propeller-driven planes. Airplanes also became a major means of transporting cargo and mail.

How a Jet Engine Works

There are three types of jet engines: turbojet, turbofan, and turboprop. All three are internal combustion engines. Jet engines draw in air and combine it with fuel. This produces powerful gases that are ignited with an electric spark. The ignited gases blast out the back of the engine. As the jets of gas shoot backward, the jet shoots forward. Early jets could reach a speed of 550 miles (885 kilometers) per hour. The fastest jet is the Lockheed SR-71 Blackbird Strategic Reconnaissance Jet. It can go as fast as 2,500 miles (4,022 kilometers) per hour.

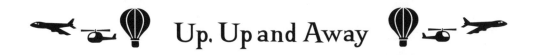

WINGSPAN: the width of a plane's wings.

MONOPLANE: an airplane with a single set of wings.

SOUND BARRIER: when something goes as fast as the speed of sound.

Aviation Firsts

- The first MONOPLANE flew in France in 1907.
- The first commercial airplane service began operating in 1914 in Florida.
- World War I was the first war in which airplanes were used. At first they were used to spy on enemy positions. By the end of the war, planes were fitted with guns and bombs.
- The first commercial airline began flying passengers in 1919 in Germany.

Breaking the Sound Barrier

Sound travels at a speed of 750 miles (1205 kilometers) per hour. Any type of movement that is faster than 750 miles per hour will break the sound barrier. On October 14, 1947, pilot Chuck Yeager became the first person to break the SOUND BARRIER by flying 769 miles (1,237 kilometers) an hour. When the sound barrier is broken it causes a sonic boom. This is a very loud booming sound.

Air Force One

Air Force One is the call sign for the plane carrying the president of the United States. A call sign identifies a person or object over a radio or other means of communication. There are two identical Boeing 747 airplanes, and both planes are called *Air Force One*, but only when the president is aboard. The presidential airplane always flies with a convoy of planes. Included in the convoy are cargo planes, and a fuel plane.

75

Air Force One is stored in Hangar 19 at Andrews Air Force Base in Maryland. In the air, *Air Force One* is like an **OVAL OFFICE** on wings. It is equipped with telephones, computers and televisions, fax machines, and photocopiers. Two kitchens are used to prepare meals for the president and other passengers. There is a conference room, a pharmacy, and a bedroom for the president. There are also desks and rooms for the presidential staff and members of the press who are flying with the president.

The 89th Airlift Wing of the United States Air Forces maintains the presidential planes that make up *Air Force One*. The air force plane that carries the vice president is called *Air Force Two*.

Interesting Facts About Presidential Airplane Flights

• The president arrives at *Air Force One* from the White House on a helicopter called *Marine One*.

• Franklin D. Roosevelt was the first United States president to fly in an airplane. His plane was a Boeing 314 Clipper and it took him to Casablanca in North Africa. There President Roosevelt met with Great Britain's Prime Minister Winston Churchill to plan the World War II Allied Invasion of Europe.

Guess what?

Mail going further than 200 miles is delivered to the airport. where it is flown to an airport closest to the postal processing station of its destination.

• Dwight D. Eisenhower was the first U.S. president whose airplane used the *Air Force One* call sign.

• Harry Truman was the first president to fly within the United States. He took a one-day trip to his home in Missouri.

• John F. Kennedy had the words United States of America painted on the presidential jet. He also had the American flag painted on each side of the jet's tail.

• Lyndon B. Johnson was sworn in as the 36th president of the United States on *Air Force One* after the assassination of John F. Kennedy in Dallas, Texas.

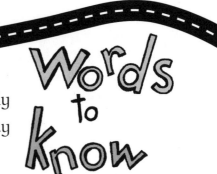

Words to know

OVAL OFFICE: the office in the White House where the president works.

VERSATILE: able to be used in a lot of ways.

VERTICAL: up and down.

MOLECULES: very small particles made of combinations of atoms.

Helicopters

Helicopters are **VERSATILE** flying machines. They can fly forwards, backwards, or side to side. They can take off and land in a **VERTICAL** position, and they can hover in the air. The rapidly spinning rotor on the top of the helicopter lifts it off the ground and into the air.

Since there is no need for the runway that an airplane needs, helicopters can be used for many things. They can rescue people and transport them to hospitals. They can deliver supplies and troops during

a battle, and swiftly take troops off the battlefield if needed. Helicopters are also used to fight fires. The world's fastest helicopter is the Lynx, which has reached a speed of 249 miles (401 kilometers) per hour.

Design Your Own Stamp

The United States Postal Service honors people and events with stamps. How do they decide who to put on a stamp? They get suggestions from ordinary citizens, like you. You could have a say in who or what is honored on a future stamp. Come up with some ideas and then choose the one you like the most. Make a few sketches of your idea. The write to the committee with your suggestion.

Citizen's Stamp Advisory Committe
Stamp Development
United States Postal Service
1735 North Lynn Street
Room 5013
Arlington, VA 22209-6432

You should send your sketch along with your suggestion. You might want to write a letter to convince them that your idea is a good one. If the committee chooses your idea, they will hire an artist to create the actual stamp. You'll have to be patient. It takes about three years for the stamp to become available after the committee has decided to use your idea.

Learn About Air Molecules

Air is made up of all different types of MOLECULES. These molecules are constantly moving. This experiment will let you experience the movement of air molecules for yourself. If the perfume doesn't belong to you, be sure you get permission to use it.

1 Open the bottle of perfume and carefully place a few drops on the cotton ball. Don't get any perfume on your hands, fingers, or clothing.

2 Place the cotton ball with the perfume in a corner of a room. Go to the opposite corner of the room and start watching the time. How many seconds or minutes does it take for you to start smelling the perfume?

SUPPLIES
→ bottle of perfume
→ cotton ball
→ clock with a second hand

The molecules in the perfume are rising off the cotton ball and mixing with the molecules in the air. Since air molecules move, the perfume molecules will eventually make their way to you and you will be able to smell the perfume. How long does it take?

Make Your Own Parachute

Parachutes are used to transport people, food, water, and medical supplies to areas where planes and helicopters cannot land. These places may be in war zones or areas affected by natural disasters. A parachute works by creating a form of resistance called drag. As the material of the parachute inflates, drag is increased and falling is slowed. Making a parachute is easy, but get a grown-up's help when you are ready to launch it.

SUPPLIES

→ 10-by-10-inch (25-by-25-centimeter) piece of plastic, such as an old plastic tablecloth

→ hole punch

→ 6-ounce paper cup

→ 4 pieces of string, each 10 inches (25 centimeters) long

3 Using the hole punch, punch four holes into the paper cup around its rim. The holes must be the same distance from each other.

1 Using the hole punch, punch a hole in each corner of the plastic.

4 Connect the plastic to the paper cup with the strings. Make sure your knots on both the cup and the plastic are strong. Ask an adult to help you launch your parachute from a deck or window.

2 Gather the plastic into a point in the middle. Punch a hole through the point so that there is a hole in the middle of the plastic.

Drop Someone a Line

In the days before email, people wrote a lot of letters and sent them through the mail. A postcard is a quick and easy way to drop someone a line.

1. Copy the postcard template. Write a short message to one of your friends on the left side of the postcard. Don't forget to sign it!

2. Address the postcard on the same side that you wrote on and add your return address. Put a stamp above the address.

3. Decorate the blank side of the postcard with crayons or markers. You can tell a story with pictures about a trip you've been on, draw something you find interesting, or just make a cool design.

4. With an adult's help, bring your postcard to the post office and mail it. Wait for a reply.

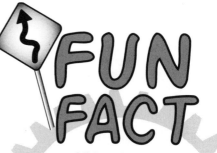

FUN FACT

Gliders have no engine, so they have to rely on a force called lift to stay in the air. Lift is produced by the glider's wings, and the faster the speed of the glider, the more lift the wings make.

Transportation of the Future

There's no doubt about it. People have come up with some amazing ways to move. But humans aren't finished looking for ways to make transportation faster, easier, and safer. What can we expect from transportation in the future?

The entire world will be moving away from using **FOSSIL FUELS** over the next few decades. Right now most transportation runs on gasoline or other products made from oil. It won't be long before we run out of fossil fuels, so the world needs to have other ways to power transportation.

Electricity will become more and more important in the transportation of the future.

The fastest wheeled train in the world is currently France's TGV, an electric train that can travel at 357 miles (575 kilometer) per hour. Electric cars that charge overnight using household electricity are available now, but they are expensive and not used by very many people yet. They can reach speeds of around 60 miles (95 kilometers) an hour and travel about 50 miles (80 kilometers) before needing to be recharged.

Future transportation may rely on a free and easily found form of energy—the sun. Sunlight can be use to make electricity, called **SOLAR POWER**. Solar cars that run on their own electricity are one possibility for mass use in the future.

Words to Know

FOSSIL FUELS: coal, oil, natural gas—fuel made from the fossils of plants and animals that lived millions of years ago.

SOLAR POWER: power made from the rays of the sun.

ELEMENT: a pure substance that cannot be broken down into a simpler substance. Everything in the universe is made up of combinations of elements. Oxygen and gold are two elements.

EQUILIBRIUM: balance.

Maglev Trains

Maglev trains run on magnetic power. Maglev is short for Magnetic Levitation. Maglev trains actually run above a single rail at speeds of around 300 miles (500 kilometers) an hour. Germany and some Asian countries are currently using Maglev technology. Many people believe that only a matter of time before all countries, including the United States, will use Maglev technology. One type of Maglev technology uses magnets both inside and outside of the train along with a source of electricity. Other Maglev technology is currently being developed.

Another possibility is hydrogen as an alternative fuel. Hydrogen is the most abundant **ELEMENT** in the universe. Hydrogen cars take water (H_2O), and break it up into hydrogen and oxygen. They use the hydrogen to make electricity to run the car, and give off oxygen and water. Not only can we use hydrogen to power our cars—the process doesn't create any pollution.

Space Travel: What's Out There?

The biggest changes in future transportation will involve moving people and cargo to outer space. NASA is the United States space agency. It stands for National Aeronautics and Space Administration. NASA is in charge of exploring and studying space for the United States.

The Human Transporter

In 2001, inventor Dean Kamen made his Segway Human Transporter available to the public. This electrically charged scooter uses human **EQUILIBRIUM** to operate it. If you lean forward, the Human Transporter will move forward. If you tilt backward, it will come to a stop. The Human Transporter can also turn around. It goes up to 12.5 miles (20 kilometers) an hour and will run for 17 hours before it has to be recharged. Some people think this might be a fast and inexpensive way to move around.

Freedom Ship

In the future, people may be looking to ships, not only for transportation, but also for housing. A floating city called *Freedom Ship*, which is in the planning stages, will be the world's largest ship. *Freedom Ship* will be 1 mile long, 3 city blocks wide and 25 stories high. Fifty thousand people will be able to live on *Freedom Ship*, while it sails around the world once every two years.

The building of the International Space Station (ISS) in 1998 was the first step in outer space transportation. Astronauts have lived in the ISS since 2000. The ISS orbits 218 miles above the earth and is as large as a football field. It travels over 17,000 miles (27,000 kilometers) per hour, and it orbits the earth 15 times a day. ISS astronauts, who have come from 17 different countries, conduct experiments and continue building and maintaining the space station. The United States Space Shuttle and the Russian Soyuz Spacecraft transport people and supplies to the ISS. Recently, a robotic Russian cargo spacecraft docked at the ISS. Space tourists have also hitched a ride on Soyuz spacecraft and visited the ISS. It's an expensive ticket—people have paid $25 million to go!

The orbits of the International Space Station and other spacecraft can often be seen from Earth. Log onto NASA's International Space Station web page (http://spaceflight.nasa.gov/realdata/sightings/) to see when a spacecraft will be flying over your neighborhood.

Humans are already traveling, working, and living in space. NASA is working on new launch vehicles called *Ares I* and *Ares V* that will return humans to the moon and later transport them to Mars and other solar system destinations. *Ares I* will launch a crew and *Ares V* will transport cargo, like the hardware needed to land on the moon. It will also carry food, fresh water, and other basic living supplies for a lengthy visit to outer space. These trips are planned to the ISS by 2015 and the moon by 2020.

Guess what

Rockets are able to propel spacecrafts into space because they don't need an outside source of oxygen. Rockets carry their own oxygen supply.

Space Travel Firsts

• The first country to travel in space was the Soviet Union (now Russia). When it sent up the robotic satellite, *Sputnik*, on October 4, 1957, the space age began.

• The first human to go into outer space was the Soviet Union cosmonaut, Yuri Gagarin, who orbited in the *Vostok 1* on April 12, 1961. His orbit lasted 108 minutes, then he ejected from the spacecraft by parachute once he was close to Earth.

• Alan Shepherd became the first American in space when, on May 5, 1961, he flew more than 200 miles up for 15 minutes.

• The first astronauts landed on the moon on July 20, 1969. Americans Neil Armstrong and Buzz Aldrin actually walked on the moon and collected moon rocks.

• The first United States Space Shuttle blasted off on April 21, 1981.

Find Polaris, the North Star

For centuries, people have looked to the North Star to guide them. Also called Polaris, the North Star always points north, so it is a reliable compass. As slaves made their way to freedom on the Underground Railroad, they used the North Star to guide them north.

To find the North Star, go outside on a dark, clear night. Locate the Big Dipper, the seven stars that look like a ladle. Find the two stars that make up the edge of the dipper that is opposite the handle. Draw an imaginary line through those two stars towards the Little Dipper, a smaller ladle. The brightest star on the end of the Little Dipper is the North Star.

Make Your Own Collage Transportation Keepsake Box

Be sure to ask permission before cutting pictures out of magazines and catalogs.

SUPPLIES
→ **magazines and catalogs**
→ **scissors**
→ **a clean box about the size of a shoe box or slightly larger**
→ **markers**
→ **glue**

1 Look through magazines and catalogs to find pictures that represent different types of transportation. Look for pictures of cars, buses, trains, boats, airplanes, animals, and people walking.

2 Carefully cut out the pictures. Cut out enough pictures to cover all sides of the box (except the bottom), as well as the cover.

3 Glue the pictures to the box. Overlap the pictures so that the box starts to look like a collage. Color any empty spaces with marker so that the box is fully covered.

4 Place your transportation collage box in a safe place to dry. Once it is completely dry, use your box to hold school supplies, craft supplies, photos, or other special things you want to keep.

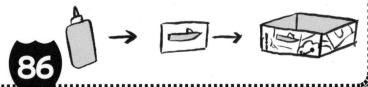

GLOSSARY

AFT: at the back.

ANCESTORS: people who came before us.

ANTARCTICA: the land around the South Pole.

ARCHAEOLOGIST: a scientist who studies ancient people and their cultures.

ASSEMBLY LINE: a series of workstations were steps in the assembly of a product are carried out by workers or machines as the product is moved along.

AXLE: a thin rod a wheel turns on.

BEAST OF BURDEN: animal that carries loads.

BERING STRAIT: the body of water that separates Russia and Alaska.

BERINGIA: a bridge of land that covered the Bering Strait during the Ice Age.

BILLOW: swell or fill with air.

BIOFUELS: fuel from something that was once alive, like plants or algae.

CANISTER: a container.

CANVAS: a strong cloth, usually made of cotton.

CARAVEL: a sailing ship with two or three masts.

CARGO: things being transported.

CEDAR: the wood from a type of tree.

CHER AMI: French for dear friend.

CHRISTOPHER COLUMBUS: the Italian explorer who discovered America for Spain while searching for a new route to China.

CIRCUMNAVIGATE: to travel around.

CIRCUS MAXIMUS: a large sports arena in ancient Rome.

CONTINENTS: the major landmasses on Earth.

CROIX DE GUERRE: "cross of war" military decoration to recognise acts of bravery in war.

DOMESTICATED: tamed.

DUNG: animal droppings or waste.

ELEMENT: a pure substance that cannot be broken down into a simpler substance. Everything in the universe is made up of combinations of elements. Oxygen and gold are two elements.

EQUILIBRIUM: balance.

EVOLUTION: changing gradually over many years.

FLAMMABLE: able to catch fire.

FOSSIL FUELS: coal, oil, natural gas—fuel made from the fossils of plants and animals that lived millions of years ago.

GRAVITY: the force that pulls objects toward each other and holds you on the earth.

GREENHOUSE GASES: gases that trap heat in Earth's atmosphere and contribute to global warming and climate change.

HACK: a type of cab, short for "hackney."

HARNESS: straps that attach a horse or other animal to a cart.

HYDROGEN: a gas that can be used as a fuel.

ICE AGE: a time in history when much of Earth was covered in ice.

ICON: something that is special and well known for a certain reason.

IMMIGRANT: someone settling in a new country.

IMPACT: hitting onto something.

INDONESIA: a country in the Indian and Pacific Oceans made up of almost 14,000 islands.

INDUSTRIAL REVOLUTION: the name of the period of time that started in the late 1700s in England when machines replaced people as a way of manufacturing.

INTERCEPTED: stopped from getting to its destination.

INTERNAL COMBUSTION ENGINE: an engine where fuel is burned inside a cylinder

INTERSECTION: where two or more streets meet.

IRON: a magnetic metal found abundantly on Earth.

KEVLAR: a manmade fireproof substance.

LANDAU: horse-drawn carriage.

LONGSHIP: light and fast boat used by the Vikings.

MAIDEN: first.

MANUFACTURING: to make large quantities of products.

MERCHANT: someone who buys and sells goods for profit.

METRIC SYSTEM: a system of weights and measures based on the meter and the kilogram.

GLOSSARY

MOLECULES: very small particles made of combinations of atoms.

MONOPLANE: an airplane with a single set of wings.

NETHERLANDS: a country in Northwest Europe.

NILE RIVER: a river in Africa that is one of the longest in the world.

NORSE: people living in Scandinavia in the Middle Ages.

NUCLEAR POWER: power produced by splitting or fusing atoms.

OVAL OFFICE: the office in the White House where the president works.

PACK ANIMAL: beast of burden.

PANTOGRAPH: a device on the roof of electric trains and locomotives for picking up electric current from overhead wires.

PAPYRUS: a paper-like substance made from plants that grow near the Nile River.

PARALLEL: two lines always the same distance apart.

PATENT: a document given to the inventor of something that protects them from someone copying their invention.

PEDESTRIANS: people walking to get from one place to another.

PHILIPPINE ISLANDS: an Asian country in the Pacific ocean near Japan and China.

PISTON: a small, solid cylinder that fits into a larger, hollow one.

PNEUMATIC: filled with air.

POTOMAC RIVER: the river that goes up to Washington, D.C., our nation's capital.

PREHISTORIC: long ago, before written history.

PROPULSION: a force that moves something.

PROTOTYPE: the first model of something new.

PROVISIONS: supplies.

RECONNAISSANCE: checking out what other people are doing.

REEDS: tall grasses.

RESIN: a sticky substance from trees.

RESPECTABILITY: a proper way of looking or acting.

ROBOTICS: the science and technology of robots.

SAIL: a piece of cloth attached to the rigging of a boat that catches the wind.

SCYTHIANS: nomadic people of ancient Iran.

SIBERIA: a region of Asia that is in Russia.

SLEDGE: a large sled pulled by animals over snow or ice, or over logs.

SMITHSONIAN INSTITUTION: a government organization that sponsors scientific research.

SOLAR POWER: power made from the rays of the sun.

SOUND BARRIER: when something goes as fast as the speed of sound.

SPROCKETS: the teeth on a wheel that engage the links of a chain.

STANDARDIZE: to make everything the same.

STOCK CAR: a regular car that has been modified for racing.

STRIDE: a step.

SUBMARINE: an underwater boat.

SUBMERGE: go under water.

SYMMETRICAL: the same on both sides or ends.

SYRIANS: people who live in Syria in the Middle East.

TERRAIN: land or ground and all of its physical features, such as hills, rocks, and water.

TRANSCONTINENTAL: across a whole continent.

TRANSPORTATION: a way of moving people and things.

TREAD: the grooves in a tire.

UNDERGROUND RAILROAD: a network of people who hid runaway slaves and helped them escape to freedom.

VERSAILLES: a large, very fancy palace near Paris.

VERSATILE: able to be used in a lot of ways.

VERTICAL: up and down.

VIKINGS: a group of people from Scandinavia.

WINGSPAN: the width of a plane's wings.

YOKE: a wooden frame for harnessing two animals to each other and to a cart or plow.

BOOKS

Benson, Joseph. *The Traveler's Guide to Pony Express.* Helena, Montana: Falcon Press, 1995.

Bingham, Caroline, and Trevor Lord. *Big Book of Transportation.* New York: Dorling Kindersley Limited, 2006.

Branley, Franklyn M. *Think Metric!* New York: Thomas Y. Crowell Company, 1972.

Brimmer, Larry Dane. *Subway: The Story of Tunnels, Tubes, and Tracks.* Honesdale, PA: Boyds Mills Press, 2004.

Carson, Mary Kay. *The Wright Brothers for Kids: How They Invented the Airplane.* Chicago, IL: Chicago Review Press, 2003.

Casanellas, Antonio. *Great Discoveries and Inventions That Improved Transportation.* Milwaukee, WI: Gareth Stevens, 1999.

Coiley, John. *Eyewitness: Train.* New York: DK Publishing, 2000.

Graham, Ian. *Amazing Machines: Mighty Cars.* Franklin Watts, 2006.

Farndon, John. *1000 Things You Should Know About Buildings and Transportation.* Broomhall, PA: Mason Crest Publishers, 2003.

Hamilton, John. *Transportation: A pictorial History of the Past One Thousand Years.* Edina, MN: Abdo, 2000.

Herbst, Judith. *The History of Transportation (Major Inventions Through History).* Minneapolis: Twenty First Century Books, 2006.

Humble, Richard. *Submarines and Ships.* New York: Viking, 1997.

Klaman, Bobbie and Kate Calder. *Travel in the Early Days.* New York: Crabtree Publishing, 2001.

Lavery, Brian. *Ship: The Epic Story of Maritime Adventure.* London: D.K. Publishing Inc., 2004.

Mattern, JoAnn. *Transportation: Yesterday and Today.* Farmington Hills, MI, 2004.

Maynard, Christopher. *I Wonder Why Planes Have Wings and Other Questions About Transportation.* New York: Kingfisher Books, 1993.

McNeese, Tim. *Conestogas and Stagecoaches.* New York: Crestwood House, 1993.

Old, Wendie C. and Robert Andrew Parker. *To Fly.* Boston: Clarion Books, 2002.

Richards, John. *The Big Book of Transportation.* London: Brimax, 2002.

Richards, Jon. *Transportation. (How Things Have Changed)* North Mankato, MN: Chrysallis Education, 2005.

Santella, Andrew. *Air Force One.* Brookfield, CT: Millbrook Press, 2003.

Steins, Richard. *Transportation Milestones and Breakthroughs.* Austin, Texas: Raintree Steck-Vaughn, 1995.

Sutton, Richard. *Eyewitness: Car.* New York: DK Publishing, 2005.

Will, Sandra. *Transportation Inventions:From Subways to Submarines.* New York: Bearport Publishing Company, Inc. 2006.

Williams, Brian. *Transportation Technology.* North Mankato, MN, 2008.

Wilson, Anthony. *Visual Timeline of Transportation.* New York: DK Publishing, 1995.

Woods, Michael, and Mary B.Woods. *Ancient Transportation.* Minneapolis: Lerner Publications Company, 2000.

RESOURCES

Web Sites

Advanced Transportation Technology Institute
http://www.atti-infoorg/

Boeing Air Force One Website
www.boeing.com/defense-space/military.af1/

Canoe History
http://www.waterspirits.com/history.html

Bicycle History
http://www.pedalinghistory.com/PHhistory.html

Famous Inventors Website
http://inventors.about.com/od/
famousinventions/Famous_Invention_
From_A_to_Z_Find_Any_Famous_
Invention.htm

History of railroads and maps
http://www.memory.loc.gov/ammem/
gmdhtml/rrhtml/rrintro.html#US

How Stuff Works: Transportation Channel
www.howstuffworks.com/transportation-chanel.htm

The Moon Landing
http://www.kidport.com/REFLIB/Science/
MoonLanding/MoonLanding.htm

NASA International Space Station Website
http://www.nasa.gov/mission_pages/
station/main/index.html

National Air and Space Museum
www.nasm.si.edu

National Railroad Museum
http://www.nationalrrmuseum.org

National Railroad Historical Society
www.nrhs.com

New York Metropolitan Transit Authority
www.mta.nyc.y.us

Roller Skate Museum
http://www.rollerskatingmuseum.com

Transportation Timeline
http://inventors.about.com

U.S. Centennial of Flight Commission
http://www.centennialoflight.gov

U.S. Department of Transportation (DOT) Research and Innovative Technology Administration (RITA) Statistics
www.bts.gov

Index

INDEX